KT-583-570

TEACH YOURSELF BOOKS

relaxation

relaxation

Richard Craze

TEACH YOURSELF BOOKS

For UK order queries: please contact Bookpoint Ltd, 39 Milton Park, Abingdon, Oxon
OX14 4TD. Telephone: (44) 01235 400414, Fax: (44) 01235 400454. Lines are open
from 9.00–6.00, Monday to Saturday, with a 24 hour message answering service.
Email address: orders@bookpoint.co.uk

For U.S.A. & Canada order queries: please contact NTC/Contemporary Publishing, 4255
West Touhy Avenue, Lincolnwood, Illinois 60646–1975 U.S.A. Telephone: (847) 679 5500,
Fax: (847) 679 2494.

Long-renowned as the authoritative source for self-guided learning – with more than
30 million copies sold worldwide – the Teach Yourself series includes 200 titles in the fields
of languages, crafts, hobbies, sports, and other leisure activities.

A catalogue record for this title is available from The British Library.

Library of Congress Catalog Card Number: On file

First published in UK 1998 by Hodder Headline Plc, 338 Euston Road, London NW1 3BH

First published in US 1998 by NTC/Contemporary Publishing, 4255 West Touhy Avenue,
Lincolnwood (Chicago), Illinois 60646–1975 U.S.A.

The 'Teach Yourself' name and logo are registered trade marks of Hodder & Stoughton Ltd.

Copyright © 1998 Richard Craze

In UK: All rights reserved. No part of this publication may be reproduced or transmitted
in any form or by any means, electronic or mechanical, including photocopy, recording,
or any information storage and retrieval system, without permission in writing from the
publisher or under licence from the Copyright Licensing Agency Limited. Further details
of such licences (for reprographic reproduction) may be obtained from the Copyright
Licensing Agency Limited, of 90 Tottenham Court Road, London W1P 9HE.

In US: All rights reserved. No part of this publication may be reproduced, stored in a
retrieval system, or transmitted in any form, or by any means, electronic, mechanical,
photocopying, or otherwise, without prior permission of NTC/Contemporary Publishing
Company.

Typeset by Transet Limited, Coventry, England.

Printed in Great Britain for Hodder & Stoughton Educational, a division of Hodder
Headline Plc, 338 Euston Road, London NW1 3BH by Cox & Wyman, Reading, Berks.

Impression number	10	9	8	7	6	5	4	3
Year	2002	2001	2000					

This book is dedicated to Julie Wootton
and Sophie, Tom and Emily, of course

About the author

Richard Craze is a freelance writer specialising in books on Chinese culture, sex, the New Age, and complementary medicine. He has some 20 books in print including:

Graphology for Beginners (Hodder & Stoughton, 1994)
Feng Shui for Beginners (Hodder & Stoughton, 1995)
Chinese Herbal Medicine (Piatkus, 1995)
The Spiritual Traditions of Sex (Godsfield Press, 1996)
Teach Yourself the Alexander Technique (Hodder & Stoughton, 1996)
The Card Playing Kit (An Eddison Sadd edition for Simon & Schuster, Australia, The Red House, UK and Elan Press, Canada, 1995)
Astral Projection – A Beginner's Guide (Hodder & Stoughton, 1996)
Hell – An Illustrated Guide to the NetherWorld (Godsfield Press & HarperCollins, 1996)
Tantric Sexuality – A Beginner's Guide (Hodder & Stoughton, 1997)
The Feng Shui Pack (Godsfield Press & HarperCollins, 1997)
Herbal Teas (Quintet, 1997)
Practical Feng Shui (Anness Publishing Ltd, 1997)
The Spice Companion (Quintet, 1997)
Feng Shui – A Complete Guide (Hodder & Stoughton, 1997)
The Feng Shui Game Pack (Godsfield Press & HarperCollins, 1997)
Teach Yourself Chinese Astrology (Hodder & Stoughton, 1997)
Teach Yourself Traditional Chinese Medicine (Hodder & Stoughton, 1998)
Chinese Horoscopes (Anness Publishing Ltd, 1997)
The Sextasy Extasy Card Kit & Book (Godsfield Press & HarperCollins, 1998)

CONTENTS

INTRODUCTION

Drinking coffee has already been shown to raise anxiety levels and blood pressure, but it may also make you lose your temper, says Marc Parmentier of the Institute for Interdisciplinary Research in Brussels. Caffeine, he explains, blocks a 'receptor' chemical in the brain which induces a calming effect on our minds. Male mice, genetically engineered to simulate the effects of regular coffee drinking, were found to be unusually aggressive.

Stress is one of the biggest factors in ill health today. Did you know that one in five companies attribute up to 50 per cent of all days taken off because of sickness to stress-related illness? Or that 100 million working days are lost each year in the United Kingdom alone? Or that 30 times as many working days are lost as a result of stress-related mental illness than are lost from industrial disputes? These facts are all work related; we don't have figures to show how many relationships fail due to stress, or how many illnesses such as heart disease, cancer and strokes can be directly attributed to stress, or even how the quality of our lives may be adversely affected by our ability just simply to ... relax.

This isn't primarily a book about stress, however; it's a book about how to combat stress. We know that stress has the potential to be extremely bad for us, to cause us ill health and seriously affect the quality of our lives. There are many books available that will tell you all about stress – its causes and conditions, but this is a practical guide to remedy the situation. In the following pages you will find many techniques and tips regarding the most widely tested methods of relaxation – methods that work and are safe, simple and easy to follow.

Some people are able to relax naturally, but the majority of us who lead busy and stressful lives may well need the odd pointer, some useful tips and hints, or a helpful suggestion or two to acquire this ability. There is a skill involved in relaxation, and maybe it is a skill that we need to relearn. We had it when we were small children but as we grow older, we lose the trick of simply switching off and relaxing. So in *Teach Yourself Relaxation* you will find many techniques of both physical and mental relaxation – techniques drawn from a wide range of disciplines such as:

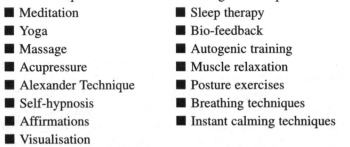

- Meditation
- Yoga
- Massage
- Acupressure
- Alexander Technique
- Self-hypnosis
- Affirmations
- Visualisation

- Sleep therapy
- Bio-feedback
- Autogenic training
- Muscle relaxation
- Posture exercises
- Breathing techniques
- Instant calming techniques

At the beginning of each chapter you will find a *'think box'*. This contains information which may not be directly beneficial to you, but may set you thinking about your general health and how research findings may have been interpreted incorrectly over the years.

Throughout each chapter you will find *action plans*. While it is not essential that you follow these action plans it has been proven that we learn better if we are involved rather than if we just read passively. If you carry out the action plans you may benefit merely from having put them into practice.

The exercises and action plans in this book assume a certain level of general good health and responsibility. However, if you are in any doubt as to your health or fitness then it is advisable to consult a qualified medical practitioner before embarking on any exercises, techniques or relaxation programmes.

This is primarily a book about how to achieve better levels of relaxation for yourself so I have included as many helpful hints and tips as space allows. I hope you will learn something useful from reading this book – even if it's just to put it under your head in a hammock and doze off in the garden on a warm summer's afternoon.

1 | WHAT IS STRESS?

You have a greater risk of heart disease if you have high levels of an amino acid called *homocysteine* in the blood than if you have high cholesterol, according to Dr Thomas Stuttaford who cites recent work at Leeds University. But, high levels of the amino acid are easily countered by taking doses of folic acid, which is readily available in liver, fresh fruit and vegetables, or in supplements such as those taken by pregnant women. The finding may explain why some people who have high cholesterol levels still seem to have some protection against heart disease. 'A rich man's diet, despite the sauces and the butter, may cause less heart disease than would be expected because it is also rich in folates, and the affluent therefore have lower levels of homocysteine than the poor,' says Stuttaford.

Flight or fight?

Imagine the situation. It is the Stone Age. You are sitting quietly in your cave when you hear a roaring from outside. It's obviously a large animal. You have two choices – fight it or run away from it. That's it: just two things you can do. This is known as the *flight or fight response* (sometimes known as the anger and fear response). Now come forward in time to the present day. You are sitting quietly in your car at the traffic lights when you hear loud hooting from behind. You have two possible responses – fight back or run away. However, fighting back is now socially unacceptable and running away means abandoning your car and possessions. So what can you do? Basically not a lot except bottle up the stress and carry on to the office where you can take it out on someone else.

Evolution

Humans, like all animals, take a long time to evolve and we simply haven't had enough time to relearn the flight or fight response. We are engineered to respond exactly as if we were still living in caves, although society has evolved, and very rapidly. When you encounter the flight or fight response your body undergoes many physical and chemical changes to prepare you for either eventuality. When you can't respond in either of these two ways your body cannot get rid of the build-up of potential energy needed to fight off an attack or to run away.

Social changes

If not attended to, this build-up can cause emotional and physical harm. This is why 'stress' is such a modern buzz word and why so much time and effort is dedicated to eradicating it. Older people might well say that in their day they didn't need stress management counselling. This is true for their day, but society is changing so rapidly that we simply can't ignore it. The rate at which information hurtles towards us is intensifying in such a way that someone from even ten years ago simply wouldn't recognise what we have to assimilate today.

Put simply, the rate at which society is changing demands that we too adapt or perish. Stress management is a way of adapting, and relaxing is a method of stress management – probably one of the best.

What happens to our bodies?

It might be useful just to look at some of the physical and psychological changes that occur to the body whenever you encounter that flight or fight response – and that's probably a few hundred times each day.

- blood pressure goes up
- heart rate increases
- breathing becomes shallow but rapid (hyperventilating)
- throat tightens
- salivation stops
- oxygen consumption increases
- less blood is supplied to the major organs

- more blood is supplied to the brain
- more blood is supplied to the skeletal muscles
- need to urinate increases
- back stiffens
- blood supply is withdrawn from outer skin
- temperature of body extremities drops
- numbness and tingling in fingers and toes
- increase in rate of sweating
- immune system is less efficient
- blood vessels dilate
- digestive process ceases
- increases in electrical activity in the brain
- adrenals excrete adrenaline, cortisol, noradrenalin into bloodstream
- liver function is impaired
- muscles tense and contract
- blood sugar levels increase
- pupils dilate
- skin becomes more dry.

These are all responses for a life-or-death struggle. How many of those do you encounter each day? Not many, I bet, but the body still responds, still prepares itself as if it was about to be seriously challenged at any moment.

Staying alarmed

If we do fight or run away quickly then your body needs all these changes, and all the excess chemicals will be burnt off and the body will return to normal. If, however, you don't do anything then these chemicals – adrenaline and blood sugars – will build up, and all the physical changes will stay in place for much longer. Only by concentrated relaxation can you return your body to normal. If you don't do something about it your body will learn to stay alarmed all the time – it's as if it thinks: 'there's not much point relaxing if I'm just going to go back to an alarmed state again immediately'.

Effects of long-term stress

If your body doesn't either work off the effects by fighting or running away, or consciously return to normal by undergoing some form of relaxation then the effects can become semi-permanent and this can cause:

- aggressive behaviour
- difficulty sleeping
- emotional instability
- overeating/loss of appetite
- excessive smoking
- excessive alcohol consumption
- accident proneness
- difficulty making decisions
- negative self-awareness
- anxiety
- depression
- phobias
- negative emotional responses – guilt, shame, loneliness, jealousy, moodiness

- apathy
- fatigue and exhaustion
- tension
- nervousness
- panic attacks
- avoidance of confrontation
- inactivity
- listlessness
- trembling
- drug taking
- insomnia
- early waking
- permanent numbness
- difficulty thinking.

And all because someone tooted at you at the traffic lights. That's right, it's as simple as that. Someone upsets you, confronts you, makes you angry and you get the full response: if you don't deal with it your body can begin to suffer any of the above effects.

Major health problems

If your body is subjected to those effects over a long time, it can suffer many instances of ill health of which the major causes are:

- heart disease
- strokes
- asthma
- stomach ulcers
- nausea

- irritable bowel syndrome (IBS)
- skin disturbances such as eczema, rashes and dermatitis
- disturbed or unusual menstrual cycles and flow
- cancer
- constipation/diarrhoea
- migraine
- headaches
- impaired vision and eyesight.

Obviously there are a great many factors that influence whether we will get any or all of these illnesses. Each of us deals with the build-up of stress in different ways. Some of us can cope with a high level of stress – and even seem to thrive on it – while others need much more ordered, regulated lives to be able to cope. Those of us who cope well may need little in the way of extra training or exercises, but those of us who cope badly will need help. This help can be learnt easily and simply.

The three skills

Those of us who cope well seem to have three things going for us:

- **Commitment** – we are dedicated to our families, hobbies, work, leisure activities, social life.
- **Challenge** – we see each opportunity as a challenge rather than a setback. We bounce back quickly and easily.
- **Control** – we feel able to cope because we feel in control. We don't feel like victims and we have a sense of direction in our lives – we know where we are going and anything that deflects us is allowed to do so for only a short while.

However, each of these three is a particular skill that can be learnt – and we will learn them in this book.

How do you know you're stressed?

I could just give you a list of symptoms and you'd read them and do nothing about it, so perhaps it's time for your first *action plan*. Answer the following questions as honestly as you can and award yourself the following points:

Never	0
Rarely	1
Occasionally	2
Often	3
Always	4

TICK BOXES AND ADD UP YOUR SCORE AT THE END	Never 0	Rarely 1	Occasionally 2	Often 3	Always 4
I feel exhausted					
I am obsessive about hygiene					
I am worried I might have a breakdown					
I can't stop obsessive thoughts and worries					
I cry easily and feel emotional					
I eat irregularly					
I feel dizzy, faint or far away					
I feel I can't cope					
I feel irritable					
I feel lethargic					
I feel life is worthless					
I feel pessimistic about most things					

I feel physically run down					
I feel pressurised all the time					
I feel short of breath					
I feel something bad will happen at any moment					
I feel tense and nervous					
I feel tension in my neck, shoulders and chest					
I get a lot of headaches and migraines					
I have constant niggling pains					
I have difficulty concentrating					
I have no friends and don't socialise					
I have no interest in sex					
I have palpitations and panic attacks					
I have sudden feelings of fear and panic					
I have trouble sleeping					
I lack confidence					

I smoke and drink too much					
I suffer from upset stomachs and have poor bowel movement					
I take drugs to help me get through the day					
FINAL TOTAL	TOTAL	TOTAL	TOTAL	TOTAL	TOTAL

When you have answered each of these questions and awarded yourself the appropriate points you can add them up and score your own stress level.

- Under 20 points   You seem to be showing no signs of stress. No action needed.
- 20–30   Mild stress. You need to look at what is causing you the stress and rectify it.
- 31–40   Moderate stress. This could be beginning to affect your health long term and you'd be advised to pay some serious attention to what is causing you the stress.
- 41–60   Above average stress. You need to both look at what is causing you the stress and do something about it, as well as having a health check-up and monitoring your long-term stress plans.
- 61–80   High stress. There is something wrong with your lifestyle and you need to do something about it immediately. The stress you are encountering is simply too high.
- More than 80 points   Very high stress. If you do not take prompt and effective action you may be at risk of serious illness from such high stress levels. Do something about it now!

What causes stress?

Once we have recognised the signs and realised that we too are suffering from the badly processed response to stress, we have to *identify the causes*. Stress management consultants use a general list of some 45 principal life events that are known to cause stress. These range from the death of a spouse (rated at 100), to a rise in mortgage rates (rated as 31), down to a minor breaking of the law (rated as 15). If you clock up a score of more than 150 in a year, chances are you will experience a downturn in health of some sort. A score of anything over 300 in one year will almost certainly lead to major health problems unless action is taken.

Knowing what is on the list is helpful as you can then try to plan in advance how many of the major changes you will make in one year, although some are beyond your control.

Death of a spouse	100
Divorce	75
Marital separation	65
Prison sentence	65
Death of someone close in the family	65
Serious injury or illness	55
Getting married	50
Redundancy or dismissal	48
Marital reconciliation	45
Retirement	44
Illness affecting close family member	44
Pregnancy	40
Sexual difficulties	40
New baby	39
Change in business	38
Change in financial affairs	38
Death of close friend	38
Change in work	37
Change in relationship with partner	36
Mortgage rate rise	31
Loss of mortgage	30
New boss	28

Children leaving home	27
Problems with in-laws	26
Winning award	26
Partner changing type of work	25
Beginning or stopping study course	23
Change in living conditions	23
Change in personal habits	22
Falling out with boss	21
Change in working conditions	20
Moving house	20
Children changing schools	19
Change in social activities	18
Change in religious activities	18
Taking out loan	17
Altered sleeping habits	17
Change in family location	16
Dieting	15
Holidays	15
Christmas	15
Minor law-breaking	15

Obviously you will not agree with all of these. For instance, most people believe that Christmas should be rated a lot higher than a mere 15 and moving house should be rated higher than 20. However, experience has shown these to be about right as an indicator. What we are interested in here are the *long-term effects*. Christmas may take its toll but it is over relatively quickly whereas the death of a close family member or a prison sentence are long-term stress factors – some of which may take years to adjust to, grieve over, or come to terms with.

Some people do cope better than others with certain changes. For example, some people change jobs frequently and enjoy the challenge, while others do it rarely and find it difficult to cope.

Draw up a list of the major stress factors that you are currently experiencing and see what you score. These stress factors are not scored as to whether they are 'good' or 'bad', but merely as to their stress content. For example, having a new baby in the house is rated as 39. Obviously a new baby is a miraculous and exciting event, but it is also stressful no matter how well the baby behaves or how adept its parents are at coping. A new baby brings changes and it is these changes that are being scored as stress factors. Good stress management is learning to cope with the changes in an effective and practical way.

Changing our reactions

Having recognised the signs and identified the causes we now move on to the next step – *changing our reactions.*

Before we can change our reactions we have to know what our reactions are. The only way to know this is to study ourselves and see how we react when faced with stressful situations. We know that the two basic responses are flight or fight.

How do you react when faced with stress? Is your basic reaction to hope it will all go away and that tomorrow will bring a better situation? Or do you rise to the challenge, meet it all head-on and forge ahead?

Stress management and counselling

There are times when the effects of stress need resolving and this may be by the simple technique of talking things over. It can be helpful to have someone listen to worries and fears without actually having to make decisions about what to do. Counselling may be proactive or not – it may help just to talk and 'get things off your chest'. Many difficulties can be overcome by a chat with a sympathetic friend or relative. If the problems are more persistent, or the friends or family are part of the problem, then help from a qualified professional counsellor may prove invaluable.

Finding a counsellor

To find a counsellor it is advisable to identify accurately and specifically where your problem areas are. It makes little sense to go to a counsellor qualified as a bereavement counsellor when your stress is work related. Some services such as Samaritans will not give advice, being there merely to listen; while others will provide practical and specific instructions as to how to overcome your problems. For instance, if your worries are sex related and you go to a sex counsellor you may be offered a tailor-made package.

Your local library will have an up-to-date list of qualified counsellors in your area and the specific objectives that they will work with. You can also obtain the same information from your family doctor who may be able to recommend a counsellor attached to their own practice.

When do you need a psychotherapist?

If the problems you are encountering seem overwhelming or too complex for a counsellor then you may need the services of a psychotherapist. These are counsellors who are trained to deal with extensive and detailed exploration and analysis of your personality. They usually have both academic and medical training in treating the mind, and counselling may also be part of the service they offer.

Trusting your therapist

Listening is the chief role of the trained counsellor who will quickly put you at your ease, allowing you to talk freely. You have to be able to feel you can trust your counsellor and that there is a natural empathy or bond between you. If you feel that your counsellor is someone who you just can't talk to, then you must find another one. You must be able to reveal your emotions and thoughts openly and in an atmosphere of safety and honesty. If you feel obliged to hold things back for fear of judgement or criticisms then you have not yet found the right counsellor for you.

Stress management and warning signs

There are various factors, which you should take into account when you are checking your lifestyle for signs of stress and stress-related problems.

Check with yourself the following 20 statements. Answer them True or False. If you answer between four and eight as False then stress may be affecting you to some extent. If you answer False to more than eight then stress could be affecting you severely and you should take prompt action.

	TRUE	FALSE
I am able to express my feelings freely		
I am experiencing love in my life		
I can discuss family problems freely with my family		
I do something just for pleasure at least once a week		
I drink three or fewer drinks containing caffeine a day		
I eat at least one well-balanced meal a day		
I exercise at least twice a week		
I feel I can organise my time well		
I get seven or eight hours' sleep a night		
I have a good network of friends and acquaintances		
I have at least one good close friend to whom I can turn		
I have enough income to meet my basic requirements		
I have some religious convictions that I believe in strongly; they give me strength		
I have some time to myself every day		
I smoke fewer than ten cigarettes a day		
I take fewer than five alcoholic drinks a week		
I take part in social activities on a regular basis		
My general health is good		
My weight is about right for my height and build		
There is at least one relative to whom I can turn in crisis, who lives within a reasonable travelling distance		
TOTALS	TRUE	FALSE

Once you have checked these statements to see how they apply to you then you can ascertain how much stress you may potentially be experiencing. If, for instance, you are able to answer True to all of them then you may feel able to enjoy a stress-free life. If you, on the other hand, answered False to all of them then you really must sort out your stress levels immediately, before your health is affected long term.

Another good way to check your stress levels is to rate your emotional responses. There are some emotions which, if we experience them on a long-term basis, can be detrimental. If we experience them only infrequently they will have no lasting effect upon our health.

Check the following emotions and see which you experience occasionally and which you experience frequently. If you are experiencing more than half of them constantly then you need to take action. Rate them for frequency, on a scale of 1 to 10, and also for intensity, on a scale of 1 to 10. Any that you experience rated at more than 5 should be taken as indicative of high stress levels.

	FREQUENCY	INTENSITY
Anger		
Anxiety		
Depression		
Desperation		
Frustration		
Guilt		
Helplessness		
Hopelessness		
Irritation		
Loneliness		
Panic		
Rage		
Restlessness		
Self-consciousness		
Feeling trapped		
Feeling unloved		

You should periodically check this list for how you have felt in the past, how you are feeling right now – and also how you expect to feel in the future, say over the next six months. If you expect to experience more than four of these emotions on a level higher than 5 or on a frequent basis then you should take action to relieve the cause of the stress.

Environmental stress

Of course, not all stress is down to you. There are some circumstances when stress comes at us from the outside world over which we have no control. In the same way that we have control over our responses (or we can learn such control), we can also exercise control over our immediate surroundings. Here are some tips to help you control environmental stress.

- ■ Reduce noise levels around you to below 85 decibels.
- ■ Work in natural light as much as possible.
- ■ Enhance air conditioning and central heating with bowls of water, good air flow, plants and ionizers.
- ■ Live in harmonious relaxing surroundings – decorate if you find your house/office too depressing or drab.
- ■ Avoid overheated bedrooms.
- ■ Avoid smoky atmospheres.

What type are you?

There does seem to be quite a lot of evidence that the type of person you are has a direct bearing on how well you cope with stress – and which types of stress are more likely to affect you. Also, the type of person you are seems to have a direct relationship with the types of illnesses you are likely to encounter.

There are two basic types of people – the As and the Bs. You probably know all about A and B types. In case you don't, a quick summary:

- ■ **A types** – impatient, aggressive, ambitious, hurrying, rushing, quick, stressed, demanding, difficult, loud, creative, leading, rousing, dynamic, confident, decisive.
- ■ **B types** – patient, defensive, relaxed, considerate, cautious, careful, following, receptive, caring, nervous, questioning, indecisive, quiet, philosophical, thorough.

Which are you? Probably a good mixture of both but most of us want to be more B than A. We all know that B types live longer, suffer fewer heart problems, less stress, fewer frustrations and setbacks because they think things through more, have a calmer outlook, are more laid back and are generally nicer people. Well it's true, but A types are more dynamic, have more excitement, and are better at solving problems, exploring, discovering, creating and leading. For some tasks an A type is better, and for some a B would be more usefully employed.

B types have their downside too – they appear to be more prone to carcinogens, more prone to neurosis and mental disorders, less likely to achieve or 'reach the top', more prone to worry and sleep disorders, more prone to dietary disorders and respiratory problems.

Is being an A bad for you?

There is now so much evidence to show that being a predominantly A type is bad for your health that if you are one you might like to do something about it. But how do you tell? Time for another questionnaire. Fill it in and if you come out as an A type you might like to go on to your next action plan.

Score 5 for Always, 4 for Usually, 3 for Sometimes, 2 for Rarely, and 1 for Never					
	Always 5	Usually 4	Sometimes 3	Rarely 2	Never 1
I am eager to get things done					
I am punctual for meetings					
I am very competitive					
I do everything as fast as possible					
I feel rushed					
I focus most of my attention on work					
I get aggressive if I am frustrated					
I get impatient if I am kept waiting					
I hide my personal feelings					
I interrupt others					
I push myself and others hard					
I try to do too many things at the same time					
TOTALS					

If you scored less than 30 you probably veer towards being a B type and are excused the next action plan. Between 30 and 40 and you are borderline A type. You probably work too hard and could do with taking things a bit easier. Do the action plan anyway. Over 40 scored and you are a classic A type. Do the action plan but try to do it slowly and take your time.

The medical evidence points to A types taking longer to get rid of the effects of a build-up of stress symptoms. However, the good news is that being an A type is not set in stone. You can learn to change – and probably should if you want to avoid heart disease.

ACTION PLAN FOR A TYPES

Be focused

One thing at a time – that should be your rule. Finish each task before moving on to the next. Learn how to say 'No'. Don't take on too much. Prioritise your work schedules and make lists so you can work through them, one thing at a time. Focus on what you are doing and stop thinking ahead to what you have to do next.

Check your goals

Examine where you are going and why. List all the things you expect to achieve and why. Question every goal. Question such things as approval, ego, self-esteem and confidence. Question the values of everything you chase and see if you might not be happier without them. And maybe you don't have any goals at all but have just been rushing headlong with whatever happens. So now is the time to make a plan. Check where you'd like to be in a year, two years and five years – and how to get there without strain, rushing or stress.

Express your feelings

Begin by thanking other people when they do you a service – say 'thank you, I appreciated that'. Talk to your loved ones about how you feel even if you feel fine about everything. Tell them so. Don't bottle up your feelings. Talk to others before your feelings threaten to explode – especially anger.

Slow down

If you can't get it all done then you are trying to do too much. Learn to take more time over things – especially things like eating, relaxing, sleeping. Allow more time for each activity. Allow more time between activities so you don't have to rush everywhere.

Stop timing time

Let time take care of itself. It doesn't need any help from you. Stop watching the clock. Try to stop wearing a watch – especially at weekends when you don't need to wear one. Stop timing everything you do. Leave more time to complete things and stop worrying if you go over the deadline – nothing really bad will happen.

Take up lesiure interests

Take up a hobby – gardening, walking, sailing. Hobbies can be productive in encouraging you to take time away from work as well as keeping you fitter and healthier. Many are also relaxing in themselves, such as painting or gardening. You may also spend time doing anything which is non-productive and totally trivial and unimportant – just for fun!

Time for you

Set some time aside each day solely and utterly for you alone. It need not be too long – anything from five minutes to an hour. But make it a time entirely for you to do whatever you want. You might choose to take a walk, read a book or just sit and do nothing – but this is your time and you can do anything as long as it is for you alone, and for fun!

Watch your temper

Note down every time you lose your temper – and why. Over quite a short period of time you will quickly identify how often you get angry and, more importantly, why. Once you know what causes the loss of temper you can modify your behaviour or avoid the situations. Losing your temper once a day has the same stress effect on your arteries as smoking 20 cigarettes a day.

Managing yourself

Once you have identified which type you are then you can plan accordingly how to be nice to yourself.

- Give yourself time off – no one else will.
- Give yourself treats – reward yourself for being you.
- Regard life more like a pleasure cruise rather than a learning experience.
- Insist on giving yourself a little fun every day.
- Look after yourself – eat well and regularly, take some exercise for pleasure, get proper amounts of sleep.

You should also make sure that your basic needs are met. We all have the same basic needs:

- **Physical needs** – warmth, sleep, food, water.
- **Security needs** – to be safe from violence, disorder, instability, chaos.
- **Emotional needs** – to be loved and to give love, to have friends, to belong to a family group.
- **Respect needs** – to be valued and appreciated, to be respected and approved of, to have status and esteem, to have self-confidence and be able to do things well so we can value ourselves.

As a child these needs are met without you having to do much about it – apart from shouting a bit if you want feeding or changing. As an adult these needs can be met with fairly minimal work but we all try to increase our consumption of these needs. We try to have more than we actually need. And it is this striving for more that causes the stress. This doesn't mean we all have to be happy with less, just that our ambitions and desires can detract from our enjoying what we do have.

Successful self-management is all about counting our blessings. Once we know that we have enough to meet our basic needs we can realise that anything else is a bonus, and if we don't achieve what we set out to do it might not affect us quite as much as we previously believed.

Should and have to

You might also like to listen to your inner voice. This is the one that urges you onwards. It primarily talks to you in terms of *should, must* and *have to*. These are the key phrases to being stressed. When you do things because you believe you *should* rather than because you *want* to, then you are going to be stressed. If you don't believe this then make a list of all the tasks you do during an average day, and see which you do because you believe you *should* rather than because you want to. This doesn't mean you change anything, you keep doing all the same tasks, but maybe you can change your attitude towards them. For example, every morning I walk my dog. Do I do this because I *must*, or because I *should*, or because I want to? Let's make it clear, the dog *has* to be walked if I'm to be able to get on with my work in peace. But it isn't a chore or a task, it's an enjoyable experience because I do it because I want to. I choose to have a dog. I believe that I have a choice; when I do things because I believe I *should* then they become stressful. I am more relaxed because I have changed my mental approach to these things.

It's not the tasks that cause stress – it's mental approach. To change your mental approach you have to understand what is going on in your mind, and to do that you have to learn to listen.

Do this now

Find a quiet place where you won't be disturbed for a few minutes and sit down in a chair. Make yourself comfortable but alert. Close your eyes and let go control of your breathing. Relax and pay attention to what is going on in your mind. Don't try to focus it – merely listen in as if to a crossed line on the telephone. Listen as if to someone else's conversation. Listen to the sort of words your mind uses. Now think about any routine task you have to do every day. Listen to what your mind says if you suggest that you won't do this task again. Does it say you've *got* to do it? *Must*? *Should*? *Have to*? Or does it say you can if you want to? Interesting? Again you don't have to stop doing anything, merely change your approach. Try it and see if it doesn't lighten your load a little.

Steps to relieve stress

Here are a few tips and hints as to what you can do to relieve stress. All these will be covered in more detail later in the book but they may give you some idea of what is to come. You need a four-point plan – awareness, control, communication, and purging.

Awareness

■ Be aware of your body. Notice if stress or tension is building up in any area. This is a useful tip if you perform any routine tasks that are likely to lead to RSI (repetitive strain injury). Try to avoid bad body-posture habits.

■ Accept that you have emotions. You are allowed to have them and to express them freely.

■ Be aware that sometimes you may have more than one emotion at a time and that sometimes these emotions may be conflicting. You are allowed to be confused about your emotions.

■ Be aware that your emotions affect your actions and that your actions affect other people's emotions.

Control

■ Be aware that it is important to learn to control your breathing, either through breathing techniques or some form of meditation, as over-breathing or hyperventilation can lead to bodily tension and ill health.

■ You have control over situations. If they are causing you stress then leave. If you choose to stay then that is your choice and that acceptance alone can alleviate your stress.

■ You have the right to say no. Be assertive in stressful situations. Exercising control can alleviate stress.

■ Concentrate on what is positive around you – even in a stressful situation it is always possible to see something positive in it.

Communication

■ If you have trouble expressing how you feel you are allowed to rehearse. Practise when you are on your own to find the right words to describe how you feel. This will make it easier when you need to do it for real.

■ Sharing your emotional feelings doesn't mean only the bad ones. It is good also to communicate when your are feeling fine and happy.

■ Get someone to listen. When you need to get something off your chest ask a friend to merely listen. Your friend doesn't have to say anything or offer any advice.

■ Be assertive. If you feel uncomfortable or annoyed or undervalued by someone then tell them – they may not have realised and can then do something about it.

■ Be prepared to listen to others without offering advice. Let others around you tell you about themselves and how they feel without making judgements – just listen.

Purging

■ Learn to let off steam without hurting anyone. Bash a pillow, smash some crockery (old stuff and in private), shout in an empty room, sing in the car loudly, scream in a place where you won't be overheard or frighten anyone.

■ Take up a physical exercise simply for the fun of it. Try a martial art, ballroom dancing, canoeing, trampolining.

■ Take up something creative and allow yourself to be not very good at it – watercolour painting, poetry, sculpture in papier mâché, origami, weaving. Remember this is merely to alleviate stress, not to get you into the New York Museum of Modern Art.

Summary

1 What is the *flight or fight* response?
2 How does it affect us physically?
3 What are the long-term effects of stress?
4 What are the signs of stress?
5 What are the three skills we need to be able to cope well with stress?
6 How do you know when you are stressed?

7 What causes you stress?
8 What type (A or B) are you?
9 How could you reduce your environmental stress?
10 Are your basic needs being met?
11 How many *shoulds* and *have tos* do you respond to?
12 What are the steps to relieve stress?
13 Do you manage yourself effectively?

2 RELAXED LIFESTYLES

Our emotional stability is the key to longevity, says George Vaillant of Brigham Women's Hospital in Boston. He claims that a personality which tends to keep a constant mood and avoids extremes of euphoria and depression is a better guarantee of long life than the avoidance of fatty foods, alcohol and other drugs. Vaillant studied the lives of 63 ex-Harvard students who graduated in 1942, and divided them into three groups: the 'squares' who showed few signs of emotion, the 'distressed' men who had wild emotional swings, and an intermediate group. By the age of 75, only 5 per cent of squares had died, compared with 25 per cent of the intermediate group and 38 per cent of the distressed group. Even when smoking and drinking habits were taken into account, 'squares' still enjoyed better health. 'A personality tendency to preserve a consistent mood that is largely free of psychological distress promotes physical health much more than exercise or eating habits,' Vaillant said.

In Chapter 1 we looked at how stress can affect us and what we can do about it. One aspect of stress management is to get people who suffer from the detrimental effects of stress to look at their lifestyle and see how they might change it so that they can be more relaxed. How well we cope with change is a good indicator of how well we process our stress. Disturbances to our routine can create stressful situations. How well we cope may be influenced by the way we were brought up. Those of us who were encouraged to reach out, to explore and to learn, and were shown approval for doing so, tend to cope better. Those of us who were discouraged, restricted, over-supervised and received little approval for adventure and exploration tend to cope less well. Our normal responses are based on our internal view of the world. If we see it as a basically good, exciting, fresh, wonderful place we will respond well to change and actively seek it out. If our internal view is somewhat dimmer and we see the world as a scary place full of danger and disturbances then we will seek routine more and find change hard to cope with as it brings fresh terrors.

Some change is easier to cope with because we can plan for it. If we change jobs voluntarily we will have gone through a process of selection first. It's the same with moving house. We know what is coming to a certain degree and can plan our lives accordingly. It's when the change is sudden and unexpected that we find it much more difficult to deal with. The sudden ending of a long-term relationship often comes as a complete shock – and is thus much harder to cope with – as is the death of someone close, accidents, redundancy or being sacked, being arrested, and illness.

The reason why these unexpected events are harder to deal with is because they unsettle our internal view of the world. They make the future uncertain; they remove our control. If we are to cope better we have to reorganise our internal view, and we have to know how we cope with change.

How do you see change?

Think about an area of your life for a moment that is changing. Take some time to answer the following questions about that area and see how you view that change.

1 What is good about this change?
2 What is bad about this change?
3 Is it exciting or dismal?
4 What do you fear about this change?
5 What is the worst-case scenario?
6 What is the best possible outcome?
7 What are the long-term negative implications?
8 What are the long-term positive implications?
9 How can you alter this change to make it better?
10 How does this change affect you personally?
11 How does this change affect the people around you?

It might be interesting to see how quickly you answer some of these questions. For instance, did you answer 5 and 7 quicker than 6 and 8? Or the other way round? If you find it quicker – and thus easier – to view this change as bad or negative it might reflect your own way of thinking about change. If you see change as something that good can come out of, it might indicate that your internal view is much more positive and that you cope better with change generally.

Altering your response to change

If you view change as something to be feared then you might benefit from doing a little work on your attitude. This will lower the stress caused by being unprepared – or at least give you something positive to do while you are coping. There are various steps you can take to adjust your response to change. Some of them are listed below.

- **Analyse the change**. You can make lists of the good and bad aspects. Brainstorm the change and see if you can't turn it into something positive. Look at what you can gain rather than at what you stand to lose.

- **Listen to your mind**. How do you greet each new change? What does your mind say? You can try talking to yourself and try to jolly yourself along a bit if you feel dismayed by change. Try saying 'oh, come on, it won't be as bad as that.' Or 'look, you survived the last change and came out all right, what makes you think this change will be any different?'

- **Be informed**. The more information you have the less scary change is. Any new change should be investigated as much as possible so you can dispense with niggling fears and doubts. Ask questions; you may not like the answers but at least you'll know.

- **Be emotional**. Change causes emotions. You have emotions like anyone else. Be prepared to express them. If you find the change scary or perplexing or negative then be prepared to say so. Get things off your chest. Don't bottle up fears.

- **Use people**. Your friends and family are there to support you. Be prepared to use them during times of difficulty, change and crisis. Don't think you'll be burdening them. It's what they are there for – as you are there for them. Use them as a support system.

■ **Accept the situation**. Change what you can change and accept the rest – it's inevitable.

■ **Remember to breathe**. During crisis and times of change we become tense. Remembering to breathe properly will allow that tension to seep away. Don't hyperventilate (see page 44).

■ **Be relaxed**. Change causes stress. You are allowed to be stressed. Thus you are allowed to take time out for relaxing. This isn't being lazy or ignoring your responsibilities. It is vital for your health. If you don't, you carry the stress into long-term conditions.

■ **Be healthy**. Make sure you eat properly during times of change. Get regular sleep, fresh air and exercise. Now, more than ever, you need to maintain your energy levels and stay fit to cope with whatever you are facing.

■ **Change means change**. When faced with sudden and momentous change you will not only have to deal with it but restructure your ordinary day-to-day routines and tasks. Learn to delegate and make sure that everyone knows you are dealing with a crisis. Make sure others don't bother you with trivia. Don't take on any more than you can cope with. Be assertive. Don't be a martyr.

Knowing your lifestyle

We will deal with some aspects of lifestyle in more detail later in this chapter. Change, when it is sudden, is stressful, but if you prepare for the change it can be exciting and challenging. Changing your lifestyle, when you have control over it and are prepared, can be wonderfully relaxing if you go about it in the right way. But before you can change your lifestyle you have to know what sort you already have. Once you know yourself well you can decide which bits you want to keep and which bits you want to change. Try to answer the following questionnaire and be honest with yourself.

Which of these sentiments best describes how you feel about the aspects of your lifestyle listed below?	Happy with	Indifferent	Not happy with	Can be changed	Can't be changed	Action to be taken
My children						
My career						
My education						
My friends						
My family						
My partner						
My sex life						
My health						
My image						
My home						
My goals						
My hobbies						
My desires						
My needs						
My finances						
My ambitions						
My transport						
My fitness						
My diet						

My spare time					
My sleep					
My holidays					
My addictions					
My habits					
My hygiene					
My outlook					
My communication skills					
My spiritual beliefs					
My memory					
My social life					
My wardrobe					
My interest in the world					
My tolerance					
My political views					
My general knowledge					
My inner view					
My dental health					

My bowel movements						
My view of the opposite sex						
My approach to change						
My approach to life						
My pets						

You may find that you tick more than one box in a section, or that you are unsure of what action to take. It doesn't matter at this stage; this questionnaire is to get you thinking, to help you to make a start on knowing yourself and what sort of lifestyle you have and want.

Taking the next step

Only when you have gone through the pretty exhaustive process of self-examination can you really know yourself. The questionnaire may highlight areas that need changing. There may be many more questions you could ask of yourself, and please feel free to add them to this list. I've given you only a few answers; there may be many more. For instance, 'My pets' could be answered in many ways. 'Are you happy with them?' may elicit the response: 'I don't have any'. But why not? Do you want some/any/one? If so, what sort? Suppose a dog: what breed? what age? pedigree or from a rescue centre? what colour? what sex? If you don't want any pets, why not? Is this a personal choice? Perhaps your partner doesn't want any? Why not? Is your lifestyle not suitable for pets? Do you have an allergy? Do you fear small animals?

     You might think this a little strange but I'll give you a case history. A young successful businessman came to me for stress management counselling, and during the course of investigation as to the nature of his stress I asked him the same question: do you have any pets? I was quite simply astonished by his reaction. He became angry and said that of course he didn't and what did I take him for? I probed a little deeper and by following the tracks of the questions found out that he was allergic – or at least was until he left home at the age of 25 – to small furry animals. He blamed the dogs and cats that his mother kept as the cause of his allergies which manifested as asthma-like attacks. I asked if he could be in the same room as small animals now and he thought he would be moderately fine about them. I asked if he could be in the same room as his mother now and, again, got a strong reaction. His mother had divorced his father and this young man had to live with her from the age of eight (when his allergies started, incidentally) which was not an arrangement he found to his liking as he had wanted to be with his father.

His allergies were not linked to the small animals at all. By asking we can sometimes reveal facts which might otherwise go unnoticed. By resolving a lot of the conflict with his mother he could allay his fears about his allergies returning and was able, eventually, to have a dog in the house. His own son was delighted.

Healthy eating

What has food to do with relaxing? Without a healthy balanced diet you're never going to achieve the right levels of relaxation. A balanced diet can improve your general fitness, restore your energy levels, nourish your skin and hair, uplift your mood, help circulation, reinforce your immune system, raise your energy levels, tone muscle and internal organs and generally make you feel better able to cope with what life can throw at you. Good healthy eating at regular sensible times is probably one of the greatest relaxations we can enjoy – and one in which we don't indulge ourselves often enough. We only have to look to the Continent and the Mediterranean countries to see what a pleasure meals can be. Here are a few guidelines to healthy eating:

- ■ Try always to eat sitting down at a table.
- ■ Don't eat alone if you can avoid it – good conversation is a marvellous appetite stimulator.
- ■ Take your time.
- ■ Enjoy your food.
- ■ Eat regularly – three main meals a day at set times and only light snacks if you really feel hungry in between.

- Reduce your consumption of mood-altering foods and drinks – sugar, salt, caffeine, alcohol.
- If you must eat snacks switch from chocolate and crisps to fruit and raw vegetables such as carrot sticks.
- Eat less fat – butter, cheese, full-fat milk, red meats, cream, fried foods.
- Eat lots of roughage – beans, cereals, peas, fruit, vegetables, pasta.
- Eat more low-fat foods – low-fat yoghurts, margarine, semi-skimmed milk, non-oily fish, steamed and baked meals rather than fried.
- Cut down on your general intake of fat.
- Eat fresh food rather than packaged, tinned, frozen or dried.
- Cut down on processed food – pies, sausages, processed meats.
- Buy organic if you can.
- Eat smaller quantities at each meal.
- Make sure you eat some fresh green salad or vegetables at least once a day.
- Make cooking and food preparation part of your lifestyle so you can enjoy the process; for instance, bake your own bread.

Leisure time

'All work and no play makes Jack a dull boy.' The *dull* in this old adage can be interpreted as listless, lacking in energy, apathetic and generally run down, rather than merely as being boring.

Work, work, work

We all need to work, to be useful and productive, creative and occupied, but why do we work? Do we work to live? Or do we live to work? Without leisure time for hobbies, outside interests and enjoyment we become very dull indeed. Recent research in America has shown that people recovering from heart attacks make better progress and have fewer subsequent attacks if they follow a three-pronged approach to life.

1 They need to learn a meditation/relaxation technique.

2 They need a belief system of some sort to support them.

3 They need to belong to a social group of some sort – and it could be as simple as going to evening classes or having a few friends drop in on a regular basis.

The evidence also suggests that if we practise these three things before we are in danger of heart attack our likelihood of living to a ripe old age is greatly enhanced. What are you waiting for?

Leisure activities

Your leisure activities could literally save your life. So what leisure activities do you have?

ACTION PLAN

■ Make a list of all the things you'd like to do but have never got round to – and list why not.

■ List all the things you have done over the last 10 or 20 years that you really enjoyed that maybe you now don't do quite so often – or not at all. Write down the reasons why you don't do them now.

■ Take one item from each list and do it now – and then work your way through each list over the next year doing them all. Go for it!

When you start listing the reasons why you haven't done the things you want to do it gets really interesting. For instance, when I was in my teens I did quite a lot of canoeing at school. I had wanted to take it up again for a long time but kept putting it off. My reasons were lack of time, lack of a canoe, lack of a suitable river, lack of motivation and lack of energy. After doing the action plan above, I bought a canoe and all the suitable equipment. It was an old second-hand canoe but I carried out all the correct checks to make sure it floated and had no leaks. I went down to a nearby river where it was safe to canoe. Unfortunately, the one thing I had failed to check was whether I actually fitted into the canoe. I didn't, and in the process of trying to get into the canoe I fell into the river, got wet, laughed a great deal and made a complete fool of myself. When I got home I realised I hadn't had so much fun in ages – and I didn't even leave the shore, but for a while I had forgotten my work, my problems, my worries, my stress.

Who are you for?

There's an old saying which might apply to your leisure activities and why you don't do them:

> *If you're not for yourself, who are you for?*
> *If you are for yourself, what are you for?*
> *And if not now, when?*

So what are you for? Surely to enjoy life, have fun, learn a little, be nice to other people – and take some time out for yourself. When? Why, right now, of course. Remember that having a social circle of some kind is positively health enhancing.

Friends

We all have our own view of what friends are for, how they should behave towards us (and us to them), how often we should see them, how close we should be, and what sort of friends we want. Social contact is important and perhaps we suffer from shyness which makes it hard for us to meet new people or maintain contact with friends. A number of things will help you to enhance your social skills.

ACTION PLAN

■ **Talk to someone.** Go out of your way to have a least one five-minute conversation with someone you barely know every day. This could be a neighbour, a work acquaintance, somebody at the bus stop, a taxi driver.

■ **You go first.** Always be the first to ask how someone is, say 'good morning', say 'hello', wave, smile, be friendly in some way. Make it a point of principle always to be the first. Don't wait for others to ask 'How are you?' Get in there first. Make a game out of it and see if you don't get a good reaction from people when you are always the first to be friendly.

- **Be positive.** When someone asks how you are, don't give them a list of all your troubles; focus on the positive aspects of your life. If you can't do that then just say that you are fine.
- **Stay in touch.** Make a list of all the old friends you haven't been in touch with for ages – and write to them now. Or 'phone them. Or drop in to see them. It's no good thinking 'Oh, I'll let them make the first move'. Refer to the second point in this action plan. Be the first to make the move. Get in touch now, and stay in touch.
- **Be a member of the human race.** Join something today. It could be an evening class, a club, a society, an encounter group, a political forum, a discussion group, a lobby group, a protest, or even a motoring organisation.
- **Do the paper work.** Keep up correspondence. Send birthday cards. Send Christmas cards. Send thank you notes. Send postcards – lots of them. You'll be surprised how many you get back and how your social circle livens up. Remember the second point of this plan. Be first.
- **Listen.** Be a good listener. After you've made the first contact and asked 'How are you?' be prepared to listen to the answer. Having a social life means caring about people.

This is how we can increase the range and variety of our social contacts, but what about those friends we have grown out of? True there are times when some social contacts have to be pruned and we are often neglectful of doing so with the result that we sometimes give time to people who are a severe drain on our emotions and time.

ACTION PLAN

- Make a list of all your regular social contacts, friends and acquaintances.
- List next to them the qualities they bring to your life.
- List how you feel about them.
- Decide if you have further time and emotional capacity for them.

- Decide if you need to prune any of them from your life.
- Decide how you intend to prune them. This may be as simple as not staying in touch. Or it may be as confronting as actually telling them that the relationship isn't doing you any good and you need to pull out. Real assertive stuff.

Accepting our friends

The important part of friendships is acceptance. We all have expectations of what our friends should be like, how they should respond to us, how they should behave towards us, how they should treat us. How many of these *shoulds* are really necessary? The key word is acceptance. For instance, I have a very dear friend who is absolutely hopeless at being on time, fulfilling promises, remembering birthdays/arrangements/meeting places. He's never in when he says he'll be. He never turns up when he says he will. He used to irritate me so much that I was seriously considering ending the friendship until it was pointed out to me that the reason he was my friend was because of all these qualities – not in spite of them. I admire his wild nature, his lack of social responsibilities, his devil-may-care attitude, his total lack of concern about social conventions. He's my friend because he is who he is and what he is. I cannot change him; I can just accept him as he is and enjoy the friendship of one of life's wilder characters. When he does turn up he's entertaining, fun, a wonderful listener, full of stories and adventures. He drives me mad. He still irritates me but I am more than happy to have him as a friend as he lives out some of the wilder bits of life for me and saves me the trouble.

Why have friends?

Part of having friends is that they can teach us so much. Both about the world and ourselves. Through our friends we have both a fun social interaction with the world and a helpful education process. Friends unlock our emotional potential in a way that our close love relationships may not. But they can also teach us much that can be of use in our relationships. For instance, we may be much more tolerant of our friends than we are of our lovers. We forgive our friends much more easily. It's useful to remember this when we are cross with our loved ones. We wouldn't treat our friends badly but we often treat our partners so. When you are a passenger in a car driven by a friend you forgive them their bad habits and say nothing, or if you do say something you tend to make a joke of it and put it nicely. When we are a passenger in a car driven by our partner or spouse who does something wrong we are much more aggressive in our criticism. We wouldn't treat our friends like it, so why are we like it with people even closer?

What our friends teach us

Our friends can teach us much. They can teach us how to be in touch with our emotions, and being in touch gives us useful skills and enhances our lifestyle and health. We become emotionally literate and this is beneficial.

People who are emotionally in touch:

- take responsibility for their actions and feelings and don't blame others
- are able to recognise their emotional patterns and endeavour to correct any negative or unhelpful ones
- are able to see clearly the most appropriate behaviour in certain circumstances and act accordingly
- can be much more discriminating about their own negative and positive qualities
- are much more in touch with their bodies and can see how their emotional responses affect their bodily functions, language and responses
- are able to express themselves in a much wider range of emotions that are suitable for all circumstances
- are much more likely to know what they want out of life and how to get it
- can be much more helpful in dealing with other people who are in crisis
- are much more skilled in communicating their emotional needs to the rest of the world.

So you can see the value of joining that evening class. In Chapter 3 we will look at types and means of physical relaxation.

Summary

1 How do you see change? As something positive or negative?

2 Are you happy with your lifestyle? What would you change?

3 Do you eat healthily? If not, why not? What could you do to change your eating habits for the better?

4 How healthy is your diet?

5 How do you spend your leisure time? What could – and will – you do to change it?

6 What are you for?

7 How do you view your friends?

8 How can you widen your social contacts?

9 What valuable qualities do your friends bring to your life?

10 Are you as supportive of your friends as they are of you?

11 Do you find time to relax regularly with your friends?

12 What benefits does being emotionally literate bring us?

3 | PHYSICAL RELAXATION

According to Dr Susan Everson of the American Public Health Institute in Berkeley, California, middle-aged men who give up hope and consider themselves to be failures are at greater risk of dying of heart disease. She claims that giving up hope has the same effect upon the arteries of a middle-aged man as smoking 20 cigarettes a day. She reached her conclusions after a four-year study into 942 men whose attitudes to life were followed and whose arteries were studied with ultrasound scans. She said that feeling hopeless could upset the balance of hormones in the body, putting people at greater risk of heart disease and strokes.

In the last two chapters we looked at some of the theory about stress and its management. In this chapter we will look at some of the ways we can physically relax. Physical relaxation is a skill that we once had as children. As adults we can sometimes forget how to do it and need to relearn it.

To learn how to relax physically it is sometimes necessary to realise where we are holding tension – and then to let it go.

Muscle relaxing

Although this is quite a long routine it is worth doing from time to time – you may even like to do it every day if you find it beneficial.

Find somewhere comfortable to sit where you can be fairly upright. Rest your hands lightly on your thighs. Keep your legs together, feet pointing forwards and flat on the floor.

Make sure you won't be interrupted for about 20 minutes. Allow yourself to relax mentally so you can enjoy this exercise. Think of a happy time in your life or a beautiful place such as a woodland or mountain or sunny meadow. When you are sure you have stopped thinking about work or your troubles you can take a couple of deep breaths and then concentrate on your body. Try to feel where you are holding any tension without actually – at this stage – tensing anything. Perhaps it is your neck and shoulders that feel tight, or your back.

Once you are ready you can begin by tensing your feet. Scrunch up your toes as tight as possible for about five seconds. Then let go. Do this for each part of your entire body in the following order.

- Feet – push down firmly – and let go
- Ankles, calves, knees – tighten using foot pressure against the floor – and let go
- Thighs – push down hard against the floor – and then let go
- Hands – clench into fists – and then let go
- Arms – tighten biceps – and let go
- Bottom – clench buttocks tightly – and let go
- Lower abdomen – push out firmly – then let go
- Stomach – hold in, push out – then let go
- Chest – expand firmly – and let go
- Shoulders – hunch your shoulders up towards your ears as far as possible – and let go suddenly
- Neck – stretch up as far as possible; pull your chin down as far as possible – and let go
- Face – scrunch up your face as much as possible (imagine you are eating a lemon) – and let go
- Jaw – clench your teeth together as hard as possible – and let go
- Eyes – screw up your eyes tight shut – and let go
- Forehead – frown as deeply as possible – and let go.

Go through this exercise in the order suggested. Basically you are just working up the body. You can, for added benefit, work your way down again. Remember to tense each muscle group for about five seconds and as tightly as you can. Remember to let go of the tension each time. As you release the tension feel what happens to the muscles as they relax. Be aware of the difference between a muscle being tensed and being relaxed.

You can also do this exercise by tightening and releasing each muscle group twice if you are very tense. Alternatively, you can do it lying down – and don't worry if you fall asleep afterwards; this proves you really are relaxed.

Follow up

When you are working – if you work sitting down a lot – you can try hunching your shoulders and letting go to relieve any tension you may be accumulating. You also could try tensing and relaxing your leg muscles while sitting watching television.

You might like to try this exercise in bed last thing at night. It is especially useful for people who have trouble getting to sleep as it relaxes the whole body.

Relaxed breathing

It may seem an odd thing to have to learn how to breathe, but you may find it necessary. It is easy to get into the habit of poor breathing techniques and quite hard to unlearn bad breathing habits, but good breathing is essential to both general health and stress reduction. The way we breathe can indicate how stressed (and thus how unrelaxed) we are. If we are relaxed we breathe slowly and from the diaphragm. This is stomach breathing and is relaxing and good for us. When we are under pressure our breathing changes: it becomes shallower and more rapid. It also moves upwards to our upper chest. We tend to tense our stomachs, making stomach breathing much harder as the diaphragm gets restricted. Upper chest breathing has several unfortunate side effects which all have a knock on effect:

- it causes the body to eliminate too much carbon dioxide;
- this alters the acidity of the blood and it becomes too alkaline;
- this causes the blood vessels in the brain to restrict and narrow;
- this slows the circulation of oxygen in the brain;
- this causes palpitations, dizziness, chest pains and faintness;
- this leads to panic attacks;
- this causes us to restrict our breathing to the upper chest area and we *hyperventilate*;

Thus the cycle carries on. Hyperventilation – or poor breathing – can be responsible for panic attacks in a lot of people, but we can do something about it.

Curing the symptoms of hyperventilation

- **Stop it before it gets worse**. Check your breathing during the day, especially if you are prone to hyperventilate or have panic attacks. Remember to keep your breathing as low down as possible, feel your stomach pushing in and out rather than your chest rising and falling. Let go of any tension in your shoulders. Do the previous exercise and hunch your shoulders up towards your ears and let go suddenly so your shoulders drop – and so does the tension.

- **Recognise the signs**. Watch out for your breathing rate increasing, your breathing becoming more shallow, sighing, a change in where you breathe (from your diaphragm to your upper chest), any tightness in your chest, any feelings of being squeezed or stifled around your ribs, any faintness or dizziness, any palpitations.

- **Take immediate action**. If you find any of the above signs then sit down immediately and concentrate on your stomach breathing. Rest your fingertips lightly together on your abdomen so you can see the movement of your stomach. When you are breathing in the right place your fingertips will spread apart. Concentrate on breathing slowly and calmly.

- **Rebreathe**. Cup your hands over your mouth and nose and take four or five breaths (slowly and calmly, of course) and rebreathe your exhaled air. Alternatively, you can use a paper bag if you prefer. Do this for four or five breaths only. It helps to lower the rate at which you are breathing out carbon dioxide.

Hyperventilation, and the possible subsequent panic attacks, set up all the same effects as severe shock and you need to treat yourself accordingly; rest, take a little warm, sweet liquid such as a cup of tea, avoid alcohol, breathe calmly and slowly, allow yourself to be emotional, allow yourself to be comforted, talk to someone who has a medical training and who is sympathetic and can help, take steps to prevent a recurring attack, and adjust your lifestyle to avoid stress.

Curing the causes of panic attacks

Recent research has indicated that there seem to be two principal causes of panic attacks. The first is an addiction to adrenaline. This is frequently suffered by athletes who have to give up rigorous training for one reason or another. It is also suffered by people from professions such as acting, where the actor is obliged to take a rest and doesn't get the usual dose of excitement or nerves or even fear at performing.

The second main cause seems to be guilt. If this is borne in mind then the panic attack sufferers can mentally say to themselves, as they feel an attack coming on, something like 'It wasn't my fault. I did nothing wrong. I am not to blame.' This has often been shown to stop an attack before it has got a hold. Guilt is one of the most negative emotions we can have – there's nothing we can do except feel bad about whatever it is that is worrying us – and there is little we can do at that moment to put anything right. Later we might make amends or find some form of adjustment, but when we are faced with a possible panic attack, say in the early hours of the morning, there is little we can do except try to avoid the onset of a full-blown panic attack.

People who have suffered recurring panic attacks who have used the 'I must not blame myself' approach have found it to be beneficial once they have isolated the reason for their guilt.

Breathing exercise

Even if you don't hyperventilate or suffer panic attacks you might like to try the following exercise which will help you to be aware of your breathing and to take more effective control over it.

1 Find somewhere quiet to sit down where you won't be disturbed.

2 Put one hand on your chest and one hand on your stomach to see where you are breathing.

3 Listen to your breathing. Breathe in and out through your nose only. If you can hear your breathing you are doing it too heavily.

4 Concentrate on breathing with your diaphragm.

5 Breathe in through your nose and out through your mouth slowly and calmly.

6 Make sure your chest doesn't rise and fall.

7 Look straight ahead and keep your eyes open.

8 Make sure the breathing movement in your body is forwards and back rather than up and down.

9 Allow a pause between each in and out breath. You can silently mouth the word 'relax' or 'calm' to help you take the pause.

10 Allow your body to relax naturally and let all tension go.

You can do this exercise several times a day whenever you begin to feel tense or notice that your breathing is becoming upper chest breathing rather than diaphragmic.

Keeping fit

You cannot really expect to be relaxed or to learn relaxation skills if you are basically unfit. A good keep-fit regime is essential to a relaxed, healthy body. Doing some form of exercise can, in itself, be relaxing as well as improving body function generally. The effects of regular exercise are:

- reduction in stress levels
- improved breathing and lung function
- lowering of blood pressure
- reduction of both fat and cholesterol in the bloodstream
- improves the body's immune system
- eases muscular tension
- causes the body to release *endorphins* (hormones) which act as natural anti-depressants
- improves the efficiency of the heart
- improves and maintains good circulation
- protects you from heart disease
- increases longevity
- improves your self-image

- builds up confidence
- increases energy levels
- strengthens all the muscles of the body
- lowers heart rate generally
- enables the heart rate to return to normal more quickly after any strenuous exertion
- improves suppleness
- increases strength
- increases stamina
- makes you more resistant to infections
- enables you to recover more quickly from illness.

Not bad for a few minutes each day doing something you enjoy. Furthermore exercise doesn't have to be a set form of work-out routines. It can be something as exhilarating as rock climbing or as calming as gardening, as social as dancing or as energetic as tennis.

Of course you can, and many people do, perform regular exercise which has no specific function except to tone the body. We will look at exercise routines a little later in this chapter. If, however, you want to combine being fitter with an activity, listed below are some general activities with their corresponding effects.

- Martial arts - good for suppleness
- Rowing – improves stamina and strength
- Football – good all-round fitness
- Squash – good all-round fitness
- Badminton – good all-round fitness
- Tennis – good all-round fitness
- Walking – good all-round fitness
- Weightlifting – improves strength
- Canoeing – good all-round fitness
- Golf – good all-round fitness
- Yoga – good for improving suppleness
- Swimming – excellent for good all-round fitness
- Cycling – good for stamina and strength
- Gymnastics – good all-round fitness

- Jogging – good for stamina
- Dancing – good all-round fitness
- Rock climbing – good for stamina and strength.

You might like to add your own activity and look at which parts of the body and body function it improves. You might also like to look at some activities you do regularly and see how little they help – driving, sitting, reading, day-dreaming, watching television, Internet surfing, having a bath, talking, and drinking beer. Perhaps you could see a way to carry on doing these activities but make them a little more fitness orientated?

Remember that a regular fitness programme of whatever sort you enjoy will bring some important benefits to your life:

- a better physical shape
- improved mental abilities
- you feel happier
- you are more motivated
- you have more energy
- you have a better appetite and fewer digestive problems.

These benefits are especially useful if you work sitting down a lot or lead a sedentary existence. Often poor digestion is either a direct result of lack of exercise or is a cause of our lack of motivation to do any exercise. The following eight movements or exercises are designed to help overweight, under-motivated and unfit people begin a gentle programme of getting fit as well as improving digestion and bowel function. They have also been found to be especially beneficial to women who have recently given birth. They enable stomach muscles to quickly and easily find their previous elasticity and shape.

They are extremely easy to follow and carry out. If you feel that you need some warm-up stretches you will find them later in this chapter following these eight movements which, ideally, should be done first thing in the morning and again last thing at night. Do them as gently as you feel able at first and gradually increase the forcefulness or energy you put into them. As you get fitter you will naturally find your motivation to improve increases and you will want to do more. These exercises will enable you to get fit, improve your digestion and help you lose weight.

Exercise 1

Hammock swing

Place a folded blanket on the floor. Lie flat on your back on the blanket. Bend both knees, soles of the feet on the floor, feet about 30 cm apart, and heels close to the buttocks. Place both hands *flat on the floor*. Now raise your hips from the floor about 5 cm. The body weight will then rest on your head, shoulders and feet. Vigorously swing your body from side to side, *keeping your shoulders flat on the floor*, in order to tilt each hip upwards alternately.

Repeat 20 times – 10 each side. Lower your hips to the floor. Rest for five seconds. This constitutes one complete cycle.

Raise again, and continue 6 cycles of 20 beats each; that is 120 swings with 6 rests.

Exercise 2

Tensing and retracting

Position yourself as in Exercise 1. Place both hands below the small of your back, palms downwards. Raise your head (chin well down), then raise your shoulders and your legs, keeping the knees stiff, the feet coming up about 30 cm to 45 cm from the floor. Your body is balanced on your buttocks and hands – the hands being placed backwards or forwards so as to regulate the balance. Try to bring your head and feet as near together as possible (keeping your back round, not hollow), until complete contraction of the abdominal muscles is obtained. Then lower your shoulders and feet simultaneously to the floor, keeping your knees stiff on the downwards movement. When your body and feet are resting on the floor, retract the abdomen fully, contracting the buttocks.

Exercise 3

Pumping

Lie flat on your back with the muscles relaxed; by muscular effort push forward the abdominal wall, then by vigorous converse movement draw in the belly. Keep your shoulders and hips firmly on the floor.

Repeat 12 times; pause, then repeat 12 times slightly quicker.

Exercise 4

Lateral press

Stand with feet some 15 cm apart, toes turned back. Bend slightly forwards from the shoulders – not from the hips. Now try to retract the lower abdomen, and, holding it retracted, lean well over to the left side forcibly, but keeping chest muscles loose. Keep your legs straight at all times, knees stiff. Reverse to exercise the right side.

Repeat 20 times – 10 left; 10 right.

Exercise 5

Stretching and squatting

Stand with your heels fairly close together; toes pointed well out; shoulders braced back and down; abdomen well in. Place your hands on your hips, thumbs towards your back. Rise on your toes; then bending your knees outwards, slowly sink to a squatting position, keeping your spine straight, until the backs of the thighs touch the calves. Then rise slowly to the starting position, straightening your knees, and bracing the thigh muscles. Pause for a few seconds, and with your knees still held straight, try to rise still further on your toes, stretching your calf muscles, and working the ankle joint fully. Repeat from 6 to 12 times.

If there is any difficulty in balancing you may hold on to the end of a bed or the back of a chair instead of placing your hands on your hips.

Exercise 6

Squeezing and arching

Kneel on a small pillow and place both hands on the floor spreading the fingers. Now, while breathing quietly, retract the abdomen fully, at the same time hollowing the back. By a further muscular effort, bring your breast bone nearer your pelvis, squeezing in the abdomen to the greatest possible extent, elbows stiff and head held steady. Start by repeating six times and aim to increase to 18.

Exercise 7

Hip roll

Stand about a metre from a low chair, chin up, feet straight and about 30 cm apart, knees locked firmly, abdomen well drawn in. Place your hands on the back of a chair, thumbs towards your back. Grasp the chair firmly. Now swing your hips to the left, forcing the left hip well out. Reverse to the right and continue the movement. Try to keep your knees stationary, or as near to being stationary as possible. The swing from the hips should be from the contracted abdomen; don't let your legs follow the line of the hip roll. This exercise should be performed from the hips, with your legs as a steady base, the muscles of your buttocks aiding in the swing from side to side. Don't bend your elbows; keep your head still.

Repeat the movement for half a minute to begin with and increase to one full minute when you feel able. Increase speed as proficiency is attained.

Exercise 8

Breathing exercise

Stand erect and easily, heels fairly close together, arms by your side, palms inwards. Fill your lungs by taking a deep, slow breath and hold it while you do the following movement.

Raise your arms outwards from your sides, keeping your palms in the same position, until you reach the level of your shoulders. Continue to raise your arms upwards, and at the same time turn your palms inwards, so that they meet overhead. Keep your elbows stiff during the whole of this movement. To complete the movement, turn your palms outwards and bring your arms down slowly and steadily to their starting position by your sides, exhaling during the downward movement. Complete the movement by a general voluntary contraction of all the muscles of expiration, so emptying your lungs as completely as possible.

Repeat 6 to 9 times.

Warm-up stretches

1 Start by standing upright with both arms held high above your head. Allow one arm to drop to one side and stretch the other arm as far over your head as you can. Bend to one side as you stretch.

2 Stand with legs apart and hands on your hips. Bend one knee forwards while keeping the other straight. Push forwards gently and feel your thighs being stretched.

3 Step backwards with one foot and keep that leg straight. Put your hands on the thigh that is projecting forwards and push down at the same time as pushing the knee forwards.

4 Stand with your feet together and stretch down your arms to try to touch your toes. This will stretch your back. Do it gently and don't over stretch.

Posture and relaxation

When we are small children we have a natural grace and good posture. As we get older we develop bad habits and poor posture. The correction of these bad habits is the basis of the *Alexander Technique* (see Appendix, page 144) and while we cannot go into too much detail here it does incorporate some useful relaxation exercises. The most beneficial is known as the *semi-supine position* (Fig. 3.1). This is a means whereby we can lie down and help to restore our good body shape as well as relaxing for a while.

3.1 The semi-supine position

The semi-supine position

Getting down into the semi-supine position (Fig. 3.2)

1 Put a couple of books on the floor and stand facing them a body's length away and one pace to the side. Let your arms hang loosely by your sides and look straight ahead. Bring one leg backwards until it is one stride behind.

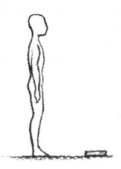

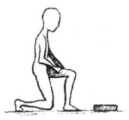
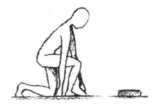

3.2   Getting down into the semi-supine

2 From this position drop down on to the rear knee. Lean forwards while still looking straight ahead and, using the arm
that is opposite the front knee, put that hand flat on the
floor in front of you and to one side.

3 Bring the other arm forwards and, as you do so, put the other
knee flat on the floor so that you are in the *crawl* position.

4 Swing your bottom over towards the space in front of the
books and let your body follow until you curl round into
the semi-supine position on your back with your knees bent
and feet raised.

5 Check that the books are in the right place and adjust your
arms so that they are correctly positioned with each hand
either side of your stomach and elbows on the floor. Make
an 'ahhh' sound and relax.

Getting up from the semi-supine (Fig. 3.3)

Basically this technique is the reverse of getting down into the semi-
supine, with one additional important point. In getting up from the
semi-supine it is important to let your eyes lead you. First, though, you
have to make a simple choice – which side to get up. You can get up to
the right or to the left, it doesn't matter which although it's important not
to get into the habit of always using the same side – keep changing.

Once you've made the decision you can get up.

1 Turn your eyes to the side you've chosen and let your head
follow. As your head turns let your body follow and roll on
to your side.

2 Keep rolling until you are back up in the crawl position.

3 From the crawl position let your eyes lead the movement –
you're body is going upwards so that's where your eyes
should be looking. Sink back on to your heels and, as you
do so, bring your arms to your side with your fingertips just
touching the floor. From this position you can go up on to
one knee.

4 From one knee, still looking upwards and forwards, you can
bring the other knee up to fall into your first step, and away
you go. You should rest your fingertips on the back of your
neck the first few times to make sure you aren't tempted to
use your arms to lever yourself up from your knees.

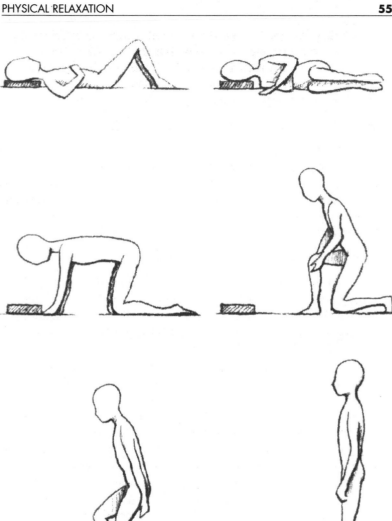

3.3 Getting up from the semi-supine position

Practise this technique in slow motion until it becomes second nature. Eventually your movements will become fluid and graceful with no strain or tension on any part of your body. Try this over the next few days to see how you get on. Remember it's no better or worse than other recommended exercises – it's just new and less damaging.

When should you use the semi-supine?

Twice a day for 15 minutes is really beneficial but if you can't do that then I would recommend that you do it for 15 minutes in the middle of the afternoon. Your muscles contract during the day as gravity takes its toll. By the middle of the afternoon you could do with *lengthening* again. Essentially, you shrink as the day goes on, so letting yourself become taller again will restore your energy levels.

What to do in the semi-supine

You'll need a friend to help you. When you're lying in the semi-supine get your friend to check the height of your head. It should be parallel and level with your spine – not at an angle up or down. Your friend should then position books of the correct height beneath your head to hold it at that height.

Next, ask your friend to check the position of your body. Your feet should be flat on the floor, parallel and about 45 cm apart. Your knees should be bent and relaxed. If they have a tendency to fall outwards move your feet slightly further apart; if they have a tendency to fall inwards move your feet slightly closer together.

Your hands should be relaxed and placed lightly one either side of your stomach. Your elbows should be touching the floor and you can *imagine* your whole torso lengthening and widening – imagine yourself as liquid: you're about to flow into a relaxed puddle. The semi-supine position lets gravity work for a while in your favour. For so long it has been pulling you downwards – now you can use it to repair some of the damage it has caused. Gravity will pull your shoulders down into a more aligned position and help your back spread openly and widely.

You can sit up from this position and lie down again to allow your back to lengthen – you may need to reposition the books.

If you want to know what your pelvis is doing while you are in this position, try putting your legs down flat on the floor and then raising them again. Feel how your pelvis swivels and tilts backwards – that's a better alignment for it than it is usually subjected to with modern living.

Using the semi-supine for relaxation

You may find this position quite exhausting at first – just lying there doing nothing can be tiring merely because it is strange. Some people find it very relaxing straight away and take to it immediately. If you've been sitting working for a while and find yourself getting tight around the shoulders, stop for a while, take up the semi-supine for a couple of minutes and feel all the tension leak away.

So now you know how to get down, get up and lie still in between. Use this position twice a day for 15 minutes each time, or as long as you feel you can to begin with, and build up. If your knees get tired you can put them down – but only one at a time and only for a few moments.

The semi-supine will correct a lot of misalignment, teach you a useful relaxation position and help your back to lengthen and widen.

Sitting, standing and walking

The Alexander Technique provides useful advice on both sitting and walking, to restore good posture and make both activities less stressful, use less energy and provide a useful means of relaxation.

Sitting down exercises

Try sitting down a few times now. Use a hard-backed chair like a kitchen chair. Obviously you have to stand up as many times as you sit down. Each time, try to feel what your head and neck are doing. Now do it again with your hands placed on the back of your neck. Lightly rest your fingertips there and feel what happens.

Does your neck tilt backwards? Can you feel yourself tensing? Most people sit down by lowering themselves into the chair using their hands or arms and, just as their bottom is about to reach the chair, they let go and fall the last inch or so. This causes the head to go back in a jerk – a startle reflex. Try sitting by lowering yourself slowly – keep your fingertips on the back of your neck – and imagine that someone is about to pull the chair away from under you. You should be able to stop at any moment because at no point do you 'let go'. You keep your balance and don't fall. This means you don't activate the startle reflex so there's no tension and you feel relaxed.

It takes some practice. Try standing up with your fingertips resting lightly on the back of your neck. It's quite hard at first attempt because the only way you're going to be able to stand up again is if you let your body fall forwards slightly. Your body will not allow itself to fall and so will propel you forwards and up (Fig. 3.4).

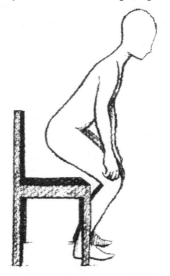

3.4   Standing up and sitting down

It's best if you do the sitting and standing-up exercise from an upright, fairly hard chair. If you try to do it from a sofa you'll have problems. However, if you want to extend the exercise to include sofas you'll have to move yourself forwards, from the sitting position, to the front edge of the sofa. That way you'll be in the optimum position to 'fall' upright.

Levering yourself up

This 'falling' upright technique can be used whenever you have to get up from a sitting position, such as getting out of bed or getting out of a car. It's worth practising these two activities. Again try doing them first as you would normally. Then put your fingers on the back of your neck and try them again. The fingers on the back of the neck have two purposes: they let you feel all the tension you would normally apply as you get up; they stop you using your hands or arms to lever yourself up. Levering is what most people do when they want to get up from a sitting position. Try getting out of a car without levering yourself; it's best if you keep your fingertips on the back of your neck. You'll find the only way to do it is to swivel round and let your legs out first (Fig. 3.5). Then you can stand up easily and gracefully. If you cannot lever yourself with your hands or arms it really is quite difficult – and yet it's something we all do. You can also try the same exercise getting in and out of bed.

Old way – one hand grips the steering wheel, the other the windscreen

New way – turn first, then stand up

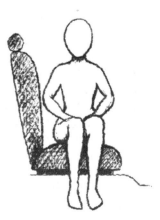

3.5 Getting out of a car

How we stand up

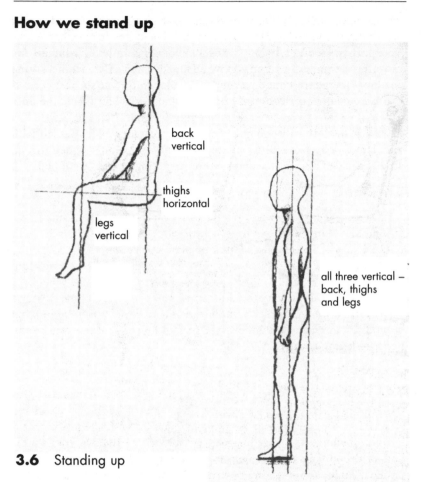

back
vertical

thighs
horizontal

legs
vertical

all three vertical –
back, thighs
and legs

3.6 Standing up

When you stand up you will notice that the actual proportion of the human body that needs to be altered to enable you to stand up is about a third. When you're sitting down you are already two-thirds standing up: your head, neck and torso are 'standing up', your lower legs are standing up, it's only your thighs that have to change position – they're the only bits sitting down (Fig. 3.6). By sloping them forwards slightly you're giving them a head start and by using your head to swing yourself forwards and up you have only to pivot your thighs through about 45 degrees. Your head, neck and torso have to move forwards but do not change their angle. Your feet and lower legs stay where they are. It's only your thighs that move. It's a simple operation that we all put too much effort into. We don't need to lever ourselves and we don't need to use up valuable energy making muscles work unnecessarily to stand up or sit down.

Walking and relaxation

There are two useful Alexander Technique guides to walking you might like to try.

Exercise 1

Next time you walk down your road, to your car, into your office – or any regular short walk you do – try to notice three things you haven't noticed before. These things might be plants you hadn't seen, a carving above a door, the colour of the windows, the pavement, the way the light changes as you enter a building, the roof line of a building. Whenever you take the same walk try to notice three new things each time. It slows your walk down and makes it more relaxing because you'll be looking around you instead of thinking ahead to your lunch, your meeting, going home or being on time.

Exercise 2

Take a walk. Take a proper walk, one in the countryside or a park, for pleasure and relaxation. As you walk imagine that there is a string attached to the top of your head and this string is pulling you gently upright. Each time you are tempted to look down or hunch your shoulders or droop your head remember the string and allow yourself to be pulled upright. Your walking posture will improve, you'll breathe better and you'll be more relaxed.

Muscles and relaxation

The two types of muscles

There are two types of muscles – voluntary (non-postural) and involuntary (postural) – and they have different qualities, characteristics, purposes, advantages and disadvantages.

- **Voluntary muscles.** These are the sort of muscles that you
  use in your arms and legs: they are flexible, they get
  exhausted quickly and they need to be directed by you.
  They are used for manipulation such as fetching or carrying,
  holding, moving and general duties. Basically they enable
  us to do things.
- **Involuntary muscles.** These are the sort of muscles that
  you have in your back: they are not as flexible as voluntary
  muscles, they can work almost indefinitely and they are
  'switched on' by the body's sensors without any input from
  you. They are used for maintaining the body's posture,
  resisting tensions and strains such as when we lift heavy
  objects and changing our shape or position. Basically they
  hold us upright.

So you can see that the two types shouldn't be confused: you use your
involuntary muscles to stand up and your voluntary muscles to hold your
newspaper when you want to read. You wouldn't expect the involuntary
muscles in your back to do the newspaper holding for you and yet you
expect the voluntary muscles in your arms to do the standing up for you.

The two systems of nerves in muscles

There are two systems of nerves in muscles. The first system has been
known about for a long time and is the system whereby the fibres in the
muscles are contracted or shortened. When the nerves stop 'firing' the
fibres are relaxed and the muscles lengthen again. The second system
has been discovered only recently and it consists of collections of nerves
that don't actually go to the muscles themselves but to lots of micro-
scopic bundles buried deep inside the muscles, called 'muscle spindles'.
They lie alongside the muscle fibres and are responsible for lengthening
the muscles. Previously we thought the muscles just relaxed when the
first system of nerves stopped firing. Now we know that there is a
second process going on as well. The second system could be likened to
a fine tuning of the muscles and the spindles have little muscles of their
own. They work to prevent the muscles over-contracting when we are
using them – a sort of shock absorber.

Poor posture

When we shorten our muscles continually without relaxing properly, the second system can become inactive and the spindles 'go dead'. This leads to a further shortening of the muscles and the result is poor posture and sagging body form.

The Alexander Technique is about lengthening those muscles again which in turn reactivates the muscle spindles and allows us to restore full muscle use and activity. People have often said that using the Alexander Technique leads to them feeling fitter and healthier overall, and 'more alive'. It's often the case that because the second system of muscle nerves has been restored to life and is working again, they feel better generally.

Research by Dr W. Barlow showed that 50 students at the Royal College of Music improved their body forms dramatically when they were taught the Alexander Technique. After only 6 months, 49 of them had increased their height by up to 4.5 cm. The muscle spindles were again working and stopping the muscles, principally the muscles in their necks, from over-contracting.

By using our bodies in the way that they were designed to be used we can gain benefits that we may not have expected as well as feeling fitter, healthier and taller.

Summary

1 **The muscle relaxing routine**

Tense then relax each muscle or muscle group in the body starting at the feet and working your way up.

2 **Relaxed breathing**

Check that you are breathing from your diaphragm and not using your upper chest. Keep one hand on your chest and one hand on your stomach to feel the out and in movement of good breathing rather than the up and down movement of poor breathing.

3 **Keeping fit**

Take regular exercise. This doesn't have to be 'exercises' – you can go dancing instead. Do the eight movements in this chapter to lead you gently into a keep-fit programme.

4 Relaxing lying down

Practise the semi-supine position advised by practitioners of the Alexander Technique.

5 Relaxing while sitting

Practise getting up and sitting down with your fingertips resting lightly on the back of your neck.

6 Relaxing while walking

Look about you, notice new things, imagine a string attached to the top of your head.

4 | MENTAL RELAXATION

Why are we [the British] less happy than we were in the 1950s? In material terms, says the clinical psychologist Oliver James, we are vastly better off than we were in 1950, when Britain was 'a world of unheated winters, rationed food and very limited pleasures'. But we're much less happy than we were then: 25-year-olds are between three and ten times more likely to suffer depression; violent crime has mushroomed; compulsive behaviour, including eating disorders, 'are at epidemic levels'. At least 20% of us will now suffer from mental illness during our lives.

The reason why we are more 'emotionally impoverished' these days, says James, is that many of us suffer from a sense of failure, a feeling which reduces the level of a chemical in the brain called *serotonin*. People who are successful and happy have high levels of serotonin; but the 'rise of individualism' in modern society and the dramatic 'increase in our aspirations' makes us feel inadequate. Those who are comfortably off are increasingly told they should be doing better. Previously oppressed people 'have come not only to believe they can enjoy unimaginable status and wealth but to regard them as entitlements'. Yet they are entitlements which society cannot deliver.

The real villain of the piece, according to James, is modern capitalism which stokes our sense of dissatisfaction and 'makes money out of disappointment'. To put it bluntly: 'Envy is at the root of modern misery.'

What turns you on?

Imagine this scenario for a moment. You come downstairs in the morning and find a letter from your bank manager saying that an unknown relative whom you have never met has died in a faraway place and left you a vast fortune. How do you feel? Excited? Happy? Now suppose the phone rings and it is the same bank manager and she says that it was all a mistake and someone else with the same name as you has really got the money. Now how do you feel? Disappointed? Depressed? Suppose the phone rings again and the same bank manager tells you that the last call was a mistake and it really is your money. Now how do you feel? Confused? Mildly elated but not sure? One more phone call, this time to say that there never was any money – it was a cruel hoax to get you to buy some insurance or to advertise some new service that the bank is offering. Now how do you feel? Angry? Let down?

The point of the above exercise is that we are all emotionally swayed by events beyond our control. In this particular case you would have experienced a whole range of emotions from joy to dismay, bewilderment to anger, and all by something that never even existed. When we are flotsam on the stream of life we can be emotionally thrown about and get pretty shaken up; when we have an emotional stability we can learn to float downstream and be a little less bumped about. Mental relaxation is a way of being more stable within ourselves emotionally.

Changing our response

Let's go back to the scenario. Perhaps when the letter arrives, if you are mentally relaxed, you might have had time to notice the tiny print at the bottom of the letter saying it was all an advertising ploy. On the other hand, perhaps you might have shrugged and thought 'Well, my life is pretty well on line anyway. This is a bonus but it doesn't affect my basic quality of life.' Perhaps, if you'd been really mentally relaxed, you might even have thought 'This could really cause problems. This isn't part of my game plan. I don't need this.' One stage further on, and you might even have laughed and thrown the letter away.

Mental relaxation is like a base camp when you go mountaineering or rock climbing. You might have adventures and excitement but it's really beneficial to have a safe place to return to, somewhere you know will always be peaceful and stable. Then when life throws things at you, you can retreat momentarily to somewhere outside the hurly-burly of the outside world.

Quick mental relaxation technique

If you encounter a stressful situation it is sometimes useful to practise this quick mental relaxation technique.

Choose a word before you start that is going to be your key relaxation word. It might be 'calm' or 'peace' or even 'nothing'. Choose only one word that will be the trigger to a relaxed mental state in the future.

■ Put one hand on your abdomen to make sure you are breathing with your diaphragm and not with your upper chest.

■ Close your eyes.

■ Take one deep breath and mentally say your key word.

■ As you hold your breath tense your shoulders; hunch them up as far as they will go towards your ears.

■ Breathe out slowly through your mouth.

■ As you do so, let go of all the tension. Let your shoulders drop.

■ While you exhale, say out loud your key word.

■ Open your eyes.

If you have time you can combine this with the muscle relaxing routine we looked at in Chapter 3.

The quick mental relaxation technique should be carried out whenever you feel you're tensing up – before the onset of real stress or hyperventilation. Obviously you won't be able to do this technique if you are driving a car or anything else that would be dangerous if you close you eyes. However, you can certainly try it without closing your eyes.

Ever had road rage?

While we are mentioning car driving, recent research has shown that a lot of people find that driving is one of their most stressful short-term situations (small children are another by the way; we will look at that later on in this book) – and one that they would most like to be able to change. We are all aware of the phenomenon known as *road rage*. Handling our anger can be a skill worth learning.

Managing anger

■ **Take responsibility**. It is your anger – no one else's. It's not a question of choosing to be angry but the fact that you are angry is all part of your make-up. There's little point saying to someone 'you make me angry because....' It is better to say 'I feel angry because....' Anger is invariably caused by our own dogma.

■ **Checking the dogma**. Most anger is caused when we are confronted. Our *shoulds* and *musts* get challenged – as do our *should nots* and *mustn'ts*. The fewer of these we have, the less we will get angry because our thinking won't be so rigid. Listen to what your inner voice is saying when you lose your temper.

■ **Appropriate anger**. Try to rationalise what level of anger is appropriate. Rate your anger on a scale of 1 to 10, mild irritation to a full blowing of your top and loss of temper. What rating would you give to your last bout of anger? Was it appropriate?

■ **The physical effects**. Notice what happens to your body when you do get angry. Notice how long it takes to return to normal. The nearer to 10 in your anger ratings the stronger and more long-lasting will be the effects.

■ **It's OK to be angry**. Sometimes being angry is an appropriate emotion. Sometimes you need to be angry. However, once you start monitoring your levels and times of anger you may find that you need to be angry less often.

■ **Let it out**. If the time or place or situation is inappropriate to being angry then don't bottle up your anger indefinitely. Talk about how you feel, calmly and rationally. Talk about your irritation before it becomes your anger. Learn to notice the warning signs of the onset of anger and learn to walk away or change your response.

■ **Be childish**. If you can't control your anger then learn to let it out in a childish but controlled way – stamp and shout in private, scream into a pillow, punch a cushion – whatever it takes to vent your feelings.

- **Pretend to be angry**. If you are being goaded to lose your temper you might like to pretend to have done so long before you actually do. This keeps everyone happy – the person goading you feels happy to have won, and you can get on with your life without the stress.
- **Forgive yourself**. It's OK to be angry. We all lose our tempers. Learn to forgive yourself afterwards – and forgive others who direct their anger at you. We are all emotional beasts and need sometimes to vent our rage. Learn to say sorry if you have lost your temper with someone. If you have overreacted to a situation then say so, forgive yourself and get on with your life. Don't dwell on past mistakes. Promise yourself to react more appropriately in future.

It's OK to be angry

The thing to remember is that it is OK to lose your temper or get cross. It is not OK to hurt, frighten or intimidate other people. We all fear that being angry will do all three. The more control we have and the less often you feel the need to be angry the healthier and more relaxed you will be. Bottling up anger probably does more harm to yourself than letting it out. Ideally not being angry at all is the best solution. If you do have problems expressing your anger it may be for one of the following reasons – think about them.

- **I have to be nice**. Sometimes we want everyone to like us and feel that losing our temper and being angry will make people think less of us and consequently like us less. However, being emotional sometimes proves you are real and people may like you even more because of it. Even if they don't like you so much at least they will have noticed you.
- **I have to be controlled**. Sometimes we fear being angry in case we go over the top and hurt someone. Learn to express your anger as irritation before it gets too bad. Learn to let out anger in a controlled way rather than blowing your top without warning.
- **I have to protect others**. Sometimes we assume too much about how other people will react. We believe that if we get

angry the other person won't be able to cope with it or they will be overwhelmed by our anger.

■ **I mustn't be angry**. It's dogma again. Who said you mustn't be angry? It's OK to be angry sometimes. You wouldn't be a human being if you didn't get angry – we all do. Getting angry is not a bad thing; it's inappropriate and destructive anger that is not OK. Hitting a pillow is fine; hitting a child is not.

■ **I mustn't upset others**. Sometimes we fear being angry in case someone will be even more angry with us – and hurt us as a consequence. This invariably stems from being punished as a child for violent outbursts. As an adult the likelihood of someone inflicting serious harm on you because you got angry is remote. The chances of you inflicting serious harm on yourself because you bottle up your anger is real.

Rigid thinking

You will notice that each of the above points begins with an *I have to* or *I mustn't*. If we have this rigid thinking we will harm ourselves. Mental relaxation is learning to let go of our dogma. Learning to be more tolerant, more flexible and more forgiving. It is better to think 'I'd *rather* they didn't do that because it irritates me' than 'they *shouldn't* do that because it irritates me'.

Listed below are 20 potential key ingredients in attaining a relaxed mental attitude.

1 **Don't take life personally**. All life is a mixture of good and bad. When bad things happen to you – as they have, do and will – accept them as part of life. They haven't been inflicted on you deliberately or as some form of divine punishment: it's just life being colourful and varied. If only good things happened we wouldn't learn anything and life would be dull. We all have a little misfortune from time to time, and we all need to work through it and learn from it.

2 **Everything changes**. Whatever your situation now it will change. There's nothing you can do so just accept that change is inescapable. When we fear change or try to avoid

it or resist it our mental processes become clogged. When we accept change as inevitable then we can react to it as exciting and our mental processes remain clear and relaxed.

3 **Stop trying to be perfect**. It is more relaxed and helpful to accept that we are human beings – full of faults and foibles. Stop thinking of yourself as a flawed being and accept the 'negative' bits as part of a well rounded personality. Accept yourself as you are. If you took away all that you consider to be 'bad' you wouldn't be the wonderful human being you are. It's OK to improve; it's unhelpful to try to be perfect.

4 **Take responsibility**. It's no one's fault you are the way you are. If you could get together everyone you blame and tell them off or punish them or rage at them, it wouldn't change a thing about you. If you blame other people or life or events you won't do anything about the way you are – you will remain a victim. If you take responsibility you can take positive steps to change anything you consider needs changing and get on with your life. Don't dwell on the past – it cannot be changed. Dwell on the future – it can be changed.

5 **Stop demanding**. Allow life to work around you rather than trying to bludgeon it into submission. Change what you can and let go of the rest. There are many things outside your control and they can be ignored. What is within your control can be dealt with.

6 **Where are you rushing to?** Life is not a destination, it is a journey. Take time out to enjoy the trip occasionally. Look around you. Count your blessings. Take some time to savour life, to enjoy the quieter bits. Put your feet up from time to time and allow yourself to do absolutely nothing except watch the scenery go by.

7 **Check the mechanics**. We are complex, fragile organisms that need a lot of care and maintenance. Look after the mechanics of your body. Without proper sleep, food and exercise it will deteriorate quicker than it should. The human body doesn't come with a maintenance manual so

you have to do a little research of your own. Be prepared for changes within your body and put right anything as it goes wrong rather than waiting until the entire system collapses. Looking after your body well isn't selfish or vain – it is sound, practical common sense.

8 **Stop banging your head on brick walls.** If you habitually encounter situations where you feel intensely frustrated and unable to change anything, maybe you should avoid them or change your response. Instead of seeing situations as frustrating try to see them as challenging. You don't have problems, you have learning experiences. You don't have frustrations, you have unique opportunities to improve your skills and abilities. There are times when we are all frustrated – we can't get what we want or get people to do what we want or get a situation to our liking – however, good mental relaxation is to do with how we handle that frustration and how we approach it. If our attitude is relaxed and we accept that frustration is inevitable we can cope better.

9 **Learn to laugh more**. Laughter, research has shown, can help us recover quicker from illness, allow us to cope better with life's dramas and generally improve our health. Check how often you laugh – not just a mere smile or chuckle but a good belly laugh, a guffawing, raucous laughter that brings tears to your eyes and has you feeling helpless – literally rolling on the floor with laughter. Go out of your way to encounter situations that you know will make you laugh. It doesn't all have to be so serious.

10 **Express your feelings**. You have them and are allowed to express them. Learn to talk more about how you feel. Be honest with others about your feelings. Don't try to protect others from them. Don't go along with others just because it makes things easier – the repercussions will be worse in the long run. Express both the positive and the negative. If you feel irritated say so. If you feel happy say so. Learn to be assertive and say when you don't want to do something or feel a situation is wrong for you.

11 **Know what you want**. Look ahead and plan where you want to be and what you want to be doing. Give your life direction. Think about yourself and what is good for you and work towards it. Don't set your sights too high but be realistic and allow for a change in plans or fortunes. Make your goals flexible. Have both long-term and short-term plans.

12 **Manage your relationships**. Unless you put in some time and effort relationships will decay and fall apart. You have to do some work. Think about your relationships – not just with your partner but also friends, work colleagues, acquaintances, close family, relatives and neighbours. If you are unhappy with any of them then work out what you can do to change them, or improve them. Be aware that all relationships are living – they grow and they wither. All relationships can end, so be prepared: nothing is for ever. If a relationship is going nowhere then it might be better to terminate it rather than let things drag on. All relationships are two-way things; you have to take the other people into consideration; they're not there just for you.

13 **Manage your time effectively**. Allow time for leisure interests, family, love, fun, work, travel, study, yourself, solitude, rest and more fun. Allot time schedules for these areas and make sure you have a little of all of them. Allow some time for future planning and to check that you are managing your time effectively.

14 **Look for choice**. There are always two ways (at least) to do anything or to approach any situation. When we have choice we feel free. When we have choice we feel in control. Accept nothing at face value. Always ask what the choices are. Look for the choices in any situation. Nothing in life is set in concrete – there is always an alternative. The alternative may not be pleasant or acceptable and we may discard it but at least we will feel as if we had a choice and thus feel freer and more in control.

15 **Develop yourself**. You are not a static being: you are growing and changing all the time. Develop new interests

and new friends constantly. Purge old interests and old situations if they no longer suit you or fulfil you. Learn to move on. When something has been done to death you can drop it. Always be ready to explore, to try new experiences, new situations. Study new things. Improve your education. Read lots. Be adaptable and eager to try anything (except incest and Morris dancing, as Oscar Wilde said). If you don't try new things you simply will have no idea if you like them or not – and don't try saying that you're not the sort of person who wouldn't like this or that – you don't know until you try. Be flexible in your thinking. Don't get stuck in routines or habits. The more unconventional, unpredictable and unstuck we are the more we develop and grow mentally.

16 **Set yourself standards**. This doesn't go against the advice about not being rigid in your thinking. We need moral standards and intellectual standards. Strive always for quality and improvement in your intellectual standards so that you remain interesting and vibrant. Set your moral standards high so you value yourself as a human being and can take pride in your achievements and moral health. Set your life standards for simplicity and happiness rather than work and acquisitions. Accept only the best for yourself.

17 **Be aware of what you are**. You are a complex being made up of emotions, physical parts, mental processes and a spiritual quality. We all need to devote some time to all four aspects of ourselves. We need to express our emotions and have lots of them; take care of our bodies and maintain them well; develop, expand and utilise our mental processes and constantly stretch them; and we need to have a spiritual dimension to our lives which doesn't have to mean belonging to an organised religion: it might be as simple as taking a delight and wonder in nature or as complicated as an entire belief system such as Catholicism or Hinduism.

18 **Be aware of who you are**. Know your limitations. Don't take on too much. Be prepared to fail occasionally.

Forgive yourself when you foul up. Laugh at yourself (a lot) when you take yourself seriously. Stop making excuses.

19 **Take stock of yourself**. Look in a mirror and see where you're at in your life. What age are you? What does that mean? How do you feel? How healthy are you? How relaxed? How much fun are you having? Do you work too hard? How are your relationships? Are you getting enough/too much sex? What are you scared of? Do you like 'you'?

20 **Be nice to yourself**. Take some time for yourself occasionally. Reward yourself, you deserve it. Treat yourself, you have earned it. Pamper yourself, you need it. Don't wait for others to approve of you, approve of yourself. Don't wait for others to love you, love yourself. Don't wait for others to take you out, take yourself out. Enjoy all you can. Have fun. Have more fun. The more relaxed we are, both mentally and physically, the better companions we are, the better we can cope with life and the better able we are to help others. The nicer we are to ourselves the more likely we are to want to be nice to others. When we are relaxed and happy others will want to be around us more.

Support systems

We all have the idea and attitude that we're supposed to do it all ourselves. We don't ask for help when we need it. If we are to take point number 20 of the above list – be nice to yourself – then we should be determined to get as much support for ourselves as we need. It is our right to be supported in problem areas of our lives and a key factor in our mental relaxation is how supported we feel – and how much support we are prepared to ask for and get.

We need to look at our attitude to support systems. Do we see them as valuable and supportive or unwelcome intervention and smothering? They may well be both, and we need to determine which is which and how to control them so they support us without interfering or limiting our potential to cope with situations ourselves. There is often a fine line between coping alone and coping badly.

ACTION PLAN

Draw a chart like the one below. List key areas in your life such as childcare, work, close personal relationships or financial matters. Answer the questions in the boxes.

Key area	What is wrong?	What support do I need?	What action can I take?	Will this help/hinder me in this key area?

We are not experts

Remember that it is not bad or wrong to seek support. We all need help and have the right to ask for it. We are not experts in all fields and we are allowed to seek the advice and help from those who are. The secret is in not accepting problem areas. Don't just put up with things and expect them to get better or improve by themselves – they often won't. It is better to accept that things are not as right as we would like them to be, and then to do something about it. If this involves asking for help or expecting support then that is a positive step, not a negative one.

What we can expect of others

We have the right to expect that others who are involved in our lives in any way pull their weight and shoulder their responsibilities. We have the right to expect their support.

In a close relationship we have the right to expect that our partner contributes as much to the relationship as we do. If we find that is not the case we cannot have a relaxed mental or emotional attitude and that causes us stress. If our partner doesn't support us in the way we would want in our relationship we have the right to find out why not, and the right to try to correct it.

There are three types of support that are invaluable in any close personal relationship.

1 **Nurturing support**. This is where your partner accepts you as you are and is kind and gentle with you. Your partner helps you find your own way by being supportive without judgement or interfering, and by co-operating with you in what you want to do.

2 **Creative support**. This is where your partner challenges and confronts you in a loving way to bring out the best in you, helping you find new levels of enthusiasm and creativity. Your partner supports you in enjoyment and fun, helping you grow and learn within the relationship.

3 **Practical support**. This is where your partner shares the tasks and work around the home or with the children so you have some time off. Your partner does a fair share and is helpful and supportive in all areas that are difficult and demanding.

If you and your partner work as a team in all three areas of support and you each give as much to the other as you receive, you are being supported. If, however, there is any of the three areas where you are not being supported you may well be being drained. In this case your mental and emotional freedom is being restricted, which prevents your total relaxation and causes stress. It is sometimes helpful to check that we are being as supported as we would want.

ACTION PLAN

Draw a chart like the one below by listing the key tasks in your life and ticking the appropriate boxes.

Key tasks	Am I being supported in this?	Is this the support I want?	Is this the support I don't want?	Is this the support I need?	Is this the support I don't need?

You will notice that there are different boxes for support you *want* and support you *need*. You have to be realistic in your expectations. You may *want* your partner to do all of the washing-up – but do you *need* this? It will make your partner irritable and you lazy. What you probably need is a fair system of sharing the washing-up and then you will both benefit.

Extending the action plan

The above action plan is not only useful for close personal relationships. You might like repeat the exercise for work, friends, leisure time and family. Once you have isolated where your problem areas are, where you are not being helped, you can source possible and potential support systems and these may include some of the relaxation therapies that you can find in the appendix.

Summary

1 Check how emotionally stable you are. Are you easily at the mercy of your emotions or are you an emotional rock?

2 Try the Quick Mental Relaxation Technique. Does it work for you?

3 How good are you at managing your anger? How could you improve?

4 What problems do you have expressing your anger?

5 Do you suffer from rigid thinking?

6 What are the benefits of flexible thinking?

7 Are your support systems in place? What do you expect of life? How could you obtain what you want? Can you differentiate between what you want and what you need?

8 Have you completed the action plan for your closest relationship? What did it tell you? How can you change anything that needs changing? Are you getting all three types of support from your partner? Do you give all three types of support?

5 | MEDITATION AS A RELAXATION

Regular jogging cannot help prevent men putting on weight in middle-age, according to Dr Paul Williams of the Lawrence Berkeley National Laboratory in California. He has studied 7,000 male joggers and discovered that they put on just as much weight between the ages of 18 and 50 as men who have never jogged, with the average male gaining 3.3lb for every decade of life. 'The perception is that people gain weight as they get older due to inactivity,' Dr Williams said. 'Our study suggests this does not seem to be the case.' He said there were physiological reasons why men put on weight as they got older, with the decline in testosterone levels a factor.

Why meditation?

Earlier in this book we talked about A and B types. Research has shown that both types tend to suffer different types of disease or illnesses. For example, A types are more prone to heart disease and strokes whereas B types are more prey to carcinogenic disorders. Stress management consultants who want to find out which type a person is (and most of us are a healthy mixture of both) predominantly use a detailed and lengthy questionnaire called *the locus of control*. This aims to highlight those of us who fall *predominantly* into either an A or B classification. These are the people most at risk from major disease. It's worth repeating that most of us fall mid-way between the two extremes and are a good balance of both, and thus are not at high risk. Those who are high-risk types need to take action.

Is there a God?

A simple way to possibly highlight which type you are is to look at how you view the universe. Do you see it as a cold, Godless place where you have to make your own breaks and there's no such thing as luck, or a place ruled by a God who dispenses luck and fate with seemingly unfathomable randomness? Basically, do you see life as something you can control or not? Those who believe life can be controlled and thus should be – every break has to be fought for; we make of it what we will; you have to get out there and take what you want from it; you make your own luck in this world – tend to be A types. Those who believe the world to be full of luck and fate and that we are somehow not in control but victims of some predetermined or destined plan over which we have no control tend to be B types.

A types tend to be people who don't believe in any form of God.

B types tend to be people who believe in some sort of God.

Remember these are the two extremes. Stress-management consultants have to find a way of bringing each of these two extremes back towards a more central middle path. It has been shown that meditation does the job for both sets of people. For A types it shows them that there might be something bigger going on in their lives than they had previously thought. For B types it shows them they may well have more control than they previously thought.

Meditation has also been shown to reduce stress levels, provide people with fairly instant calming techniques, provide suitable relaxation, lower blood pressure and generally improve a person's outlook on life – and all for the sake of a few minutes' sitting and meditating.

What is meditation?

Someone once said that if prayer was talking to God then meditation was listening to the answer. Chamber's dictionary says that meditation is to 'reflect deeply; to engage in contemplation; to consider deeply; deep thought'. It has been likened to a turning-off of the mind; wiping the slate clean for a moment or two. It is also used as a tool in seeking religious understanding; a path to enlightenment; a means of finding 'oneself'; part of a spiritual ritual for ecstatic communication with some form of divinity. In a way none of these are what we are interested in. We are looking at meditation as a means of relaxation.

How should you meditate?

There are many forms and types of meditation from the difficult to the surprisingly simple. If we are looking for a useful tool to aid relaxation we can discount some of the more bizarre and extreme forms such as Zen meditation which involves sitting cross-legged a few inches from a white wall and staring at it for long periods – up to 16 hours in some cases – without moving and barely breathing. We can also discount anything that has a religious connotation as we can discount anything that involves changing one's lifestyle; having to believe in anything; having to adopt unnatural bodily positions; having to wear anything unusual or coloured strangely; having to adopt any means whereby our friends, colleagues or family might think we had gone barking mad; having to change our diet to one of extreme veganism; having to shave our heads; having to shut ourselves away in retreats for weeks on end; having to chant, dance, whirl, fast, be celibate, be teetotal, be covered in dust or ashes, travel to faraway places, give up social contact, get up early in the morning, remember long 'mantras', follow religious teachers or gurus, go without sleep, indulge in unnatural practices of any kind – and lastly we will avoid any forms of meditation which involve bells, candles, 'hippie' clothes, incense or drugs.

So what's left?

Surprisingly quite a lot. Meditation in its purest and simplest form is easy to do, involves none of the above, confronts nobody, is enjoyable and beneficial, and is practical.

Simplicity is always the answer with meditation. As soon as it starts getting complicated or having any strange rituals attached to it, it ceases to be meditation and becomes something else. The following techniques should be simple and easy to remember as well as being safe, practical and 'normal'. Please feel free to try as many or as few as you like. If you enjoy them, do them. If you don't, then don't do them. It really is as simple as that.

Music meditation

■ Find somewhere comfortable to sit where you won't be disturbed. Close you eyes and listen to your favourite melodic piece of classical music. Sorry, but this simply doesn't work with loud rock or pop music so no Meatloaf, I'm afraid.

■ As the music plays allow your thoughts to come freely to you. Don't try to control them or channel them. Simply listen and see where your thoughts lead you.

■ Let the music wash over you. You may find this easier if you use stereo headphones. When the music finishes enjoy the silence for a while and feel how relaxed you are.

Walking meditation

■ Go for a walk in the countryside or a park on your own. This is a walk with no purpose apart from relaxing. You aren't walking your dog or going anywhere in particular. You aren't exercising or getting fit. You are going to go for a walk purely and simply to relax.

■ Don't look around you particularly but try to focus ahead so you can see where you are going but are not looking at anything in particular.

■ Let thoughts come to you but always try to remember that you are walking to meditate.

■ Feel the motion of your body through the countryside and be aware of the feel of the air on your face, the smells, the sense of being outdoors.

■ Allow your breathing to be relaxed; diaphragmic rather than upper chest. Occasionally take a deep breath to free up any tension you may have.

■ Allow about 20 minutes several times a week to walk purely for pleasure and relaxation with no other purpose – the dog can wait until later.

Breathing meditation

■ Find somewhere to sit comfortably where you won't be disturbed.

■ Let your hands fall naturally into your lap and close your eyes.

■ Allow all the tension in your neck and shoulders to drop away. You might like to shrug your shoulders up to your ears and then let them drop.

- Concentrate on your breathing. Breathe in through your nose and out through your mouth. With each in-breath mentally say the word 'calm'; with each out-breath mentally say the word 'relaxed'.
- Breath for about ten minutes like this and then slowly return to normal life and see how relaxed you feel. You can do this meditation on the train, in the office, waiting for a bus, while watching television or even in the bath. If anyone interrupts you and you don't want to say you were meditating you can just say you were thinking deeply or daydreaming.

Heartbeat meditation

- Find somewhere comfortable to sit where you won't be disturbed.
- Place you left hand on your upper chest.
- Bring your right hand round so that you can feel the pulse in your left wrist with your right index and forefinger.
- Close your eyes and feel your pulse.
- Count the pulse at the same time as you allow your breathing to drop to your diaphragm and become relaxed.
- When you are counting your pulse start to count your breathing as well.
- Unless you cheat it is almost impossible to count both breaths and pulse at the same time but it absorbs your mind wonderfully for a while, allowing deep relaxation to take place.

Forehead meditation

- Find somewhere to sit comfortably where you won't be disturbed.
- Close you eyes and look at the inside of your forehead.
- Try to imagine a small ball of blue light there.
- Concentrate on this area for about five or ten minutes and feel what it does to your overall relaxation.

Deep-breathing meditation

■ Find somewhere to sit comfortably where you won't be disturbed.

■ Place your hands on your diaphragm so that your fingertips are just touching.

■ Concentrate on diaphragmic breathing.

■ With each in-breath your stomach should expand and your fingertips part. With each out-breath your stomach should contract and your fingertips come back together again.

■ Concentrate on the movement of your fingers for five or ten minutes.

Tasting meditation

■ You can do this one anywhere and with your eyes open or closed, although it works best with them closed.

■ Fold your tongue back until it touches the roof of your mouth. With the tip of your tongue explore the sensation of the roof of your mouth. What can you taste? What does it feel like? Try it with your teeth together. Swallow if you need to.

■ After you have explored the sensations for a while allow your tongue to become still, just resting lightly on the roof of your mouth. Concentrate on this for five minutes or so and then stop.

Prone meditation

■ Find somewhere to lie down quietly where you won't be disturbed.

■ Lie flat on your back with your arms by your side.

■ Imagine that you are an inert body – completely relaxed and without movement.

■ Allow your breathing to become still and slow from your diaphragm.

■ Close your eyes and imagine you are floating.

■ Let your body become as light as a feather.

■ Stay like this for ten minutes and then return to normal.

Total relaxation meditation

- Find somewhere to lie down where you won't be disturbed.
- Lie flat on the floor with your arms by your sides.
- Close your eyes.
- Carry out the muscle relaxation programme outlined in Chapter 4 starting with your feet and working your way up your body.
- When you get to the top of your head imagine the relaxation radiating from you to the surrounding air.
- Imagine the floor beneath you to be totally relaxed.
- Imagine yourself cocooned in a bubble of relaxation.
- Imagine that this bubble will go with you when you get up again.

Object meditation

- Find a small object that you like – a statue, an apple, a child's toy, an *objet d'art*, a pebble, a lichen covered twig.
- Place it in front of you and look at it closely, carefully. Notice every small detail that you can.
- Close your eyes and see the object in your mind.
- Notice, again, every small detail.
- Open your eyes and look at the object again. What can you see now that you didn't notice before?
- Close your eyes and again see the object in your mind.
- Keep doing this for about ten minutes and you should find it relaxing.

Picture meditation

- Find your favourite picture. It could be a landscape or a still life or a beautiful portrait.
- Prop it up in front of you and look at it carefully.
- Close your eyes and see the picture again.
- Slowly allow the picture to vanish in your mind until you are left with only the frame containing white.
- Concentrate on the white in the frame for a few minutes.

- Open your eyes again and see the picture in reality.
- You might like to try this one several times.

Listening meditation

- Find somewhere quiet where you won't be disturbed.
- Sit down in a comfortable chair with your feet flat on the floor.
- Place a cushion in your lap and rest your elbows on it.
- Reach up and gently place a thumb in each ear and allow the other fingers to rest lightly on the top of your head.
- Listen to the sounds coming from inside your body – your breathing, your heartbeat and the blood pumping through your body.
- Stay like this for as long as you want to or until your arms become uncomfortable. You may have to lean slightly forwards to get really comfortable. You can also try this one propped up in bed last thing at night just before going to sleep. If you sleep alone you don't have to explain anything but if you have a partner you may have to explain what you are doing and ask not to be disturbed until you have finished – or better still invite your partner to join you and do it together.

Counting meditation

- Find somewhere to sit comfortably where you won't be disturbed.
- Close your eyes and concentrate on your diaphragmic breathing.
- Begin to count slowly to yourself.
- At the count of 'five' take one breath.
- At the count of 'ten' take another.
- Continue until you reach '100'. Then begin again.
- As your breathing becomes more relaxed and slow so should your counting – and vice versa.

The aim of meditation

If the aim of meditation is to still the mind then giving it something else to do – such as counting or reciting a word over and over – will work wonders. How complicated you want that 'something else' to be is up to you. You may like to learn an Indian phrase which is the basis of Transcendental meditation; use a phrase such as 'God is Love' (a Christian meditation); 'peace', 'calm', counting, breathing, whatever you find works for you. The object is to still the mind. If you listen quietly to what your mind is saying to you – your inner voice – it will often be telling you that you are in the wrong place at the wrong time doing the wrong thing. That's exactly what it is meant to do. It's there to protect you, to keep you from being off guard.

Distracting your mind

Meditation is not designed to eradicate the mind but to distract it. By meditating we can switch off – or not listen for a while. Sometimes that inner voice can seem to be shrieking at us and perhaps we don't need that level of being alert to possible dangers. By switching off we can relax and find a little inner peace.

Do you already meditate and not know it?

You may already be meditating and not know it. There are many forms of meditation that require no conscious effort – just a quietening of the mind. There are many things you could be doing and meditating at the same time. It is just the focus that shifts a little. If you ordinarily do certain things that occupy your mind perhaps you might like to try them but be aware that your mind is being occupied. Therefore you can achieve quite deep levels of relaxation and meditation. Here are some examples:

- gardening
- doing jigsaws
- playing chess
- jogging
- walking
- playing backgammon
- playing cards
- reading
- writing
- watching television
- daydreaming
- driving
- bathing
- washing-up
- vacuuming
- sewing

- knitting
- mowing lawns
- playing golf
- cooking
- working out in a gym

Safety and security

All of the meditation techniques described are designed to be carried out in the safety of your own home (or safely in a park with your eyes open) so that you can feel secure. If you feel secure your inner voice can be distracted in complete safety because no harm can come to you. Meditating in a crowded place full of strangers is much more difficult because your mind will certainly, and quite rightly, be on guard against potential disaster befalling you. Likewise meditating at the top of a mountain is relatively easy because you are freed from dangers. However, it isn't practical to climb a mountain every time you feel a little stressed. As someone once said 'anyone can be at peace on top of a hill, what I want is a method of finding peace in Babylon'. Hopefully some if not all of these techniques will work for you in your own personal Babylon.

A word of caution

Your mind, that inner voice, has been used to prattling endlessly to you all of your life. It may not take too kindly to being ignored for the first time, and it may well throw up some interesting diversions for your entertainment. For instance, as soon as you sit down to meditate you'll invariably find your bladder needs emptying – or at least it feels like it until you try to do so and find it doesn't need emptying at all because you emptied it only five minutes ago.

You may close your eyes and see human faces. Don't worry, it's just your mind filling in the darkness with some distractions. Some of the visual nonsense that your mind throws up can be quite alarming unless you remember that it's just your mind being petulant and childish. Ignore it.

You may find that you've forgotten to turn the cooker off (you haven't but your mind will persuade you that you have). You may feel too cold, too warm, too uncomfortable, too sleepy, too awake, too busy, too hungry (common one this), or too thirsty.

Your mind may tell you that meditating is silly or too much like hard work (it isn't at all but your mind will invent lots of reasons why it might be), or that you are too old/young to do it, or that it's only for hippies/religious people/New Agers, or that you are too grown up for this sort of nonsense. Whatever tricks your mind dreams up to stop you meditating, it's as well to be warned beforehand and then it becomes quite amusing to see the twists and turns it takes. Just be patient and give it something else to do and don't give in to its childishness. Meditating is safe, easy, beneficial, practical, healthy and therapeutic. You can come to no harm doing it and it can only relieve stress.

Summary

1 Meditation should be done somewhere safe but accessible.

2 Be as comfortable as you like.

3 Nothing about meditation should confront you or cause you to change your lifestyle, dress, diet or religion.

4 Practise for only a few minutes each day at first and build up slowly.

5 If you like a technique and it works, do it. If you don't like one or it doesn't seem to work for you, don't do it.

6 There are no rules about meditation – whatever works for you is fine.

7 Meditation is about switching off for a moment or two – it is not about being spiritual or religious although it may lead you to powerful revelations about yourself and your place in the universe – or it may not.

6 | UNWINDING

Drinking can help middle-aged women stave off the menopause, according to Dr David Togerson of the University of York. A study of 2,000 Scottish women has revealed that female teetotallers aged between 45 and 49 are four times as likely to enter the menopause as women who have at least one [alcoholic] drink a day. 'What we found was quite a difference,' Dr Togerson said, 'and issues like social class and smoking did not alter the association. The conclusion we came to was that women who consumed the least alcohol were more likely to be post-menopausal.'

We have looked at a lot of the theory relating to how and why we get stressed, as well as at some ways of becoming more relaxed. A lot of people say that they don't have a problem relaxing but rather of unwinding. So in this chapter we will look at some of the ways we can unwind together with why we might be 'wound' in the first place. Let's start with a good night's sleep.

Getting-to-sleep problems

This seems to be the problem most people have difficulty overcoming. Below are a few tips for getting to sleep quickly and easily.

Here are a few 'do's'

- Take a warm (not hot) bath before going to bed.
- Have a warm milky drink.
- Listen to soothing music as you go to sleep.
- Make sure your bed is comfortable – renew the mattress if it is over five years old.

■ Make sure you adopt a good sleeping position. Lying on your back can cause you to snore; having too many pillows can place strain on your neck muscles; lying face down with your head turned to the side can cause cramp in the neck muscles which can give you headaches. Evidence suggests that lying on your side is best with the pillow pulled into the angle between your neck and shoulder. Your legs should be slightly bent with one in front of the other.

■ Make sure your room is quiet – double glaze the windows if necessary.

■ Make sure you have enough fresh air – leave a window open.

■ Make sure you go to bed to go to sleep and not to eat, watch television or to quarrel with your partner.

■ Carry out the muscle relaxation exercise in Chapter 4 before sleep.

■ Try meditating in bed before you go to sleep.

■ Don't just lie there – if you can't sleep after half an hour get up and go and do something relaxing like having a warm bath or reading.

■ Try doing simple mental exercises – take two random letters and think of all the pop stars or film stars or books starting with those two letters, or try to remember all the names of the people in the same class as you at school.

■ Read something soothing and relaxing – no horror novels!

■ Take a little gentle exercise before getting into bed (see the eight movements in Chapter 3).

■ Take a little gentle exercise in bed – having sex is a good way of getting to sleep (afterwards).

■ Have a ritual and routine for going to bed – always at the same time and in the same way.

■ Keep a notebook and pen beside your bed so that you can jot down anything you need to remember, if you wake during the night.

And here are a few 'don'ts'

■ Don't eat a heavy or spicy meal less than three hours before going to bed.

■ Don't drink alcohol for a few hours before going to bed if you have problems getting to sleep.

■ Don't drink coffee just before going to bed (or tea or other drinks containing caffeine).

■ Don't drink a lot before going to bed – empty your bladder before retiring.

■ Don't nap during the day if you have trouble getting to sleep at night.

■ Don't go over your problems in your mind before trying to get to sleep.

■ Don't go to bed too late – go before you are over-tired (and fractious).

■ Don't go to bed too early – before you are properly tired.

■ Don't go to bed too soon after finishing your daily tasks – make sure you have a little time to relax and unwind first.

■ Don't go to bed trying to remember things you have to do tomorrow – make a list and then go to bed.

Continuous tiredness

Each time we change our pattern of life for whatever reason we will encounter stress, for instance moving house or changing jobs. This stress can cause us to feel permanently tired. We simply don't have the energy to overcome the tiredness and can become exhausted without doing much at all. If you feel that this situation is happening to you here are a few practical things you can do.

■ Make sure you are getting enough sleep and that you can get to sleep easily and quickly (see above).

■ Go to bed at the same time each day no matter what is happening in your life – things can wait until tomorrow.

■ Establish patterns of life that you can stick to – have a satisfying and nutritious regular breakfast even if you don't have time to have a sensible lunch.

■ Make sure you are getting a little gentle exercise each day (see the eight movements in Chapter 3).

■ Avoid tobacco and alcohol.

■ Avoid too much coffee and stimulating drinks.

■ Avoid drugs of any sort.

■ Make lists.

■ Stop worrying – it doesn't achieve anything. If you have worries ask for more information.

■ Stop thinking it won't get any better – it will; everything changes.

■ Keep a diary to check your progress. You may find you are improving and hadn't noticed.

■ Distract yourself with a little fun and enjoyment.

■ Ask for help and support – you deserve it and have a right to it.

■ Be kind to yourself – don't expect too much of yourself and give yourself room to fail – you are not perfect.

■ Stop dwelling on worst-case scenarios – it might never be as bad as you think.

■ Make a list each day of things to do. At the top of the list put something you have already done – even if it's getting out of bed. The next two items should be things you have to do or were going to do anyway – such as have breakfast and have a wash. The next three items should be simple things that you can do easily. The next item should be something you enjoy doing – and want to. Then add one difficult thing or something you have been putting off. Seeing your list 90 per cent crossed off will motivate you to tackle the last item.

Managing your time

Part of managing your tiredness is managing your time. If you rush around like a headless chicken not really getting anything done but consuming vast amounts of energy you will get exhausted. By managing your time you can become effective and focused, resourceful and controlled. Much better.

How much time have you got?

We have only a limited amount of time each day so it is best if we are clear about what we will spend or squander that time on. Good time management means setting goals and being realistic about them. It is also about valuing time – not squandering it on things we have no control over or cannot change.

- **One task at a time**. Finish each thing before you move on to the next. Don't start anything unless you can finish it.

- **Have a clear picture of what you are doing**. Knowing what the end should be or look like is important. If you are working haphazardly you cannot be focused.

- **Be organised**. Make and keep lists. Keep a filing system for everything – including household bills and tasks. Write down everything you need to know, remember, think about, plan and resource, on notepads. Keep a notepad by the bed, by the phone and in the kitchen. As you think of things to do or remember write them down.

- **Set deadlines**. Allot yourself time to finish tasks that is both realistic and attainable. Be aware of the deadlines and adjust your speed accordingly.

- **Don't put it off**. Do it now – not tomorrow. Be ruthless about procrastination.

- **Prioritise your time**. Know how important each task is and do the most important first.

- **Don't do it all yourself**. If you have a family make sure that they are pulling their weight. Keep household chore rotas. Even the youngest can be found something useful to do – it's good for them and good for you. Delegate as much as you can – it's not lazy, it's good time management.

- **Know when you work best**. Perhaps first thing in the morning; perhaps last thing at night. Whenever it is allot tasks to that time that are important or difficult. Times when you know you work less well you can keep for less important or easier tasks.

- **Schedule failure**. Allow a little time built into each task for disappointment, failure, being let down or having to delay. Then when things do go wrong you can cope instead of feeling you have failed personally rather than because time got the better of you or other people let you down.

- ■ **Plan time for yourself**. You are the brains behind the outfit – no matter what the outfit is (mainly yourself). Allow a little time each day for fun and enjoyment. This isn't laziness – it's healthy, therapeutic and essential. Without rest and relaxation the brain will seize up.

- ■ **Be assertive**. Learn to say 'no' and mean it. Finish what you are doing before attending to the needs of others. Be firm with yourself about finishing things or procrastination. Be assertive with others and make sure you are in control of your own time.

- ■ **Build in time off**. Into any plan, build in some time for holidays, days off and breaks.

- ■ **Be strict about weekends**. Weekends are for you and your family if you have one (unless you're scheduled to work anyway). Be strict with yourself and don't take work home or turn on the computer.

- ■ **Be strict about finishing times**. Finish when you said you were going to.

- ■ **Know your time**. Allocate the proportion of your time you think you should spend working, resting, socialising, playing and relaxing. Make sure it is realistic and stick to it.

- ■ **Find ways to speed things up**. Always be on the lookout for ways to get things done quicker – especially routine tasks that take up a lot of time and aren't particularly productive.

Being ready

Obviously none of the above will be of much use to you unless you are healthy and relaxed enough in the first place – ready to relax. Some people say they can't relax because they have a headache, illness, pain, difficult people around them, or emotional stress. We will look at emotional stress in Chapter 7 but we can take a quick look at the other problems now. Perhaps you will find some tips to help you relax.

Difficult people

They are all around us, those difficult people. They're the ones who stop us from relaxing or finding life tolerable – or are they? Perhaps it is we who allow them to interrupt us, to distract us, to anger us, to irritate us, to confront us, to upset us and to make us unhappy. The only way to find out how we relate to those we consider to be difficult people is to monitor our response and look at how and why they are difficult.

Make a list of all those you consider difficult or who, in your opinion, distract you from being relaxed – this could be your boss, your mother, your nextdoor neighbour, an old friend, your evening class teacher. Next to their names put why it is that you think each is difficult with you. Do this objectively as if you weren't involved. Then add how you respond, which could be one of three different ways.

■ I feel attacked by this person. This may be physically, psychologically or emotionally.

■ I feel rejected by this person. This may be emotionally, intellectually or physically.

■ I feel unable to communicate with this person.

Are they all different or is there a pattern emerging? If it is a pattern then you may be contributing more to their difficult behaviour than you realised. If there is no pattern and your list of names is short you may genuinely have encountered difficult people. In the first instance you may have to do some work on yourself to see why you are encountering this pattern. In the second instance you may be able to take some steps to help.

There are various ways you can deal with difficult people. Each situation is different but you may find something useful here that you may not have tried or thought of previously. You may dismiss some of these ideas as being impractical – they may well be but at least you will have exercised some control and choice.

■ Allow yourself to be overwhelmed by these people.

■ Accept this situation as unchangeable.

■ Respond in kind.

■ Be firm. State your objections and see what happens.

■ Ignore them.

- Acknowledge them and move on.
- Change your response to their behaviour to be more amenable.
- Try to get them to change their attitude to you by changing your approach to them.
- Ask a third person for help or advice.
- Delay responding until you have had time to think, adjust, cool down, meditate, plan or retaliate.
- Try to see things from their point of view – perhaps they have an agenda different from yours.
- Are you being provocative? Could you change your attitude to them?
- Sit down with them and explain how you feel and ask for their help or advice.
- Pretend to get angry to see what happens.
- Respond bizarrely to throw them off the scent.
- Move to another part of the country so you never have to meet them again.
- Bully them into behaving better.
- Try to find out why they are difficult. This may mean having to work closer with them for a while to get to know them better or spend more time around them.

Being healthy

I hope some or one of the above will work. But how about you? Are you happy and healthy enough to relax?

Let's look at a few things that may stand in the way of relaxation.

Headaches and migraines

Possible causes

- **Hormones**. Any change in the balance of hormones can contribute to headaches – these changes can include menstruation, the menopause, the contraceptive pill, any prescribed medication that contain hormones.
- **Tension**. Being hunched over a desk for too long; driving; computer work; unusual exertion.

- **Environment**. Loud noise; excessive heat; excessive cold; lights too bright/not bright enough; stuffy, badly ventilated rooms; smoky atmospheres.
- **Hunger**. Missing meals; blood sugar levels too low; too long between meals; poor diet; poor digestion.
- **Trigger foods**. These may include the known migraine triggers such as chocolate, cheese, coffee and oranges, but causes may also be nuts, tea, alcohol, any dairy products, artificially sweetened or flavoured drinks, 'E' additives, fried food, any citrus fruit, red wine.
- **Too much food**. Food eaten in overly large quantities or too quickly can trigger headaches, as can too much activity after a heavy meal.
- **Sleep**. Not enough or too much sleep, or irregular sleeping patterns may be a factor.
- **Over-exertion**. Not just after a heavy meal but too much exercise at any time can trigger a headache, especially if you are not used to it or unfit.
- **Stress**. Being angry, tense, tired or frustrated and trying to resolve personal relationship problems can be causes of headaches as can any undue stress or worry.
- **Physical causes**. There may be a medical reason why you have headaches beyond a certain limit and it would be as well to have your symptoms checked by a qualified medical practitioner.

So what can we do about them? Try some or all of the following techniques.

- **Check your diet**. Prevention is better than cure. If you know you are sensitive to certain trigger foods then avoid them.
- **Manage your stress**. Keep stress levels as low as possible. Follow the tips outlined in this book.
- **Acupressure**. Hold your right hand in front of you with the palm facing the floor, then bend your hand back slightly so that a crease appears at your wrist. Remember where this crease is, and relax your hand. Now measure the width of

two left thumbs (about 5 cm) back from that crease towards your elbow, and begin pressing deeply between the two arm bones (the radius and ulna), in line with your middle finger. You're probing for the small hollow or depression between these two bones. When you find the tender spot, massage gently and do the same to your left forearm. If this fails to work try the acupressure point slightly further up (see below).

■ **Acupressure point 2**. Press about 5 cm down from your elbow (towards your hand) on the outside (hairy side) of your upper forearm. Probe deeply in the muscle until you feel a tender spot. It will be quite tender even with only moderate pressure. Massage both arms until you feel relief from the headache.

■ **Relax**. Place a hot water bottle (warm – not hot) on the back of your neck and a warm towel on your face. You could also try a cold flannel on your temples.

■ **Soothing smells**. Try a few drops of lavender aromatherapy oil in your warm bath or burn a little in an aromatherapy burner. You could try massaging a little lavender oil into your temples.

■ **Massage**. Try massaging your temples gently and the back of your neck. You could ask a friend to massage your whole face or your neck and shoulders for you. Don't move your head around in wide circles to relieve tension or a headache; try little circles instead – tiny movements.

■ **Darkness**. When all else fails go into a dark room and lie down.

Pain

If you suffer from constant or recurring pain then trying to relax can be hard. The following techniques may help you.

■ **Know your pain**. Keep a record of when your pain is at its worst and best so you can monitor when your 'good' periods are. Try to see patterns in your pain diary so you may be able to isolate pain triggers. Try to be most active during your 'good' periods.

- **Set yourself goals**. Have a plan of action but be realistic. Try to set small goals so you will feel you are conquering a lot each time you reach one.
- **Be active**. Don't allow yourself any time to sit around and focus on your pain. Try to distract yourself if you feel the onset of pain.
- **Visualisation**. Try to imagine the pain as something hot that you can visualise being cooled down – or something cold being heated, or heavy or wet – whatever suits you best.
- **Breathe**. Try not to tense up when in pain as it affects your breathing. Likewise dropping your breathing from upper chest to diaphragmic can relieve pain.
- **Don't always be jolly**. When people ask how you are you don't always have to say that you are fine. You are allowed to express your pain when you need to.
- **Don't be a martyr**. Ask for help when you need it. Ask for support if you want to. It's OK, you're allowed to!
- **Go for it**. Simply go for whatever it is that gets you through without worrying about what other people might think or say. It's your pain and how you manage it is up to you.

PMS

Pre-menstrual syndrome (used to be called pre-menstrual tension until it was realised that it wasn't just tension) affects some 90 per cent of women, and the effects can be shattering. The symptoms can be physical, emotional or both and there are some techniques worth learning to relieve them.

- **Be kind to yourself**. During such a time be especially nice to yourself (or your partner) and make allowances.
- **Learn to recognise – and remember – the symptoms**. It might be helpful to monitor your monthly cycle and mark in your diary certain dates when you might have PMS. You can then try to take things easier, warn people, be kinder to yourself, plan your day accordingly.
- **Check your diet**. Some foods may trigger PMS more often than others. Watch out for a lack of minerals and vitamins especially magnesium, calcium, vitamin B6 and vitamin A.

■ **It's not a disease**. Learn to accept that PMS is part of a natural cycle and that there is no 'cure'. You may always have symptoms – the trick is to alleviate them rather than blame them or hate them.

■ **Be healthy**. Follow a healthy diet, exercise regularly, sleep properly and rest as much as possible.

■ **Be assertive**. If you need something to help you relieve the symptoms then ask for it. It may be time and space and they are yours (or your partner's) by right. No one should be expected to endure PMS without help or support.

■ **Check your lifestyle**. You may be stressed anyway and the underlying causes of your stress could be looked at and dealt with before tackling the PMS which may ease as a consequence.

■ **Acupressure for relieving PMT**. Once you've found and triggered a good point properly, several things may happen. You may feel a sudden sense of warmth or perspiration. You may feel light-headed or, rarely, a brief touch of nausea. These are perfectly normal acupressure reactions and simply serve to indicate you've triggered one of the better points for your problem. Then, after a few seconds of massage, check your PMT symptoms. They should be nearly or totally gone. If you've applied acupressure properly, you should get near-total relief. Suffering often vanishes completely and immediately, as if it never existed.

To find acupressure point 7 – Measure the width of one hand (about 7.5 cm) up from the bony bulge of the inner ankle (medial malleolus). The point is found alongside the shinbone (tibia), or in the space between the shinbone and calf muscle. Massage until you feel relief, working on both legs.

To find acupressure point 9 – Measure down your leg the width of one hand below the bottom of the kneecap. Slightly to the outside (lateral side, in the direction of the little toe) of the ridge of the shinbone, you should discover a long, vertical trough or valley separating the shinbone and the front of the calf muscle. Acupressure point 9 is found in that depression. Massage until relief is felt. Work on both legs.

To find acupressure point 10 – Measure the width of two thumbs (roughly 5 cm) above the most prominent crease of the inner wrist (in the direction of the elbow), in line with your middle finger. Probe between the tendons in your lower forearm. The point should ache when you contact it – not twinge sharply, as some other points (notably point 7) might.

■ **Have a baby**. Bit drastic this one but be aware that after having a baby most women report a considerable lessening in their PMS symptoms when their monthly cycle starts again. Obviously having a baby sets up lots of different sorts of stress factors but if you were going to anyway ...

ACTION PLAN

Promise yourself that you will do at least three of the following over the next month (you can do all of them) – and add at least three of your own that are not included here.

■ Take a bath by candlelight.

■ Buy a hammock and use it.

■ Read at least one popular 'trashy' novel just for fun.

■ Go to the cinema and watch a film that you wouldn't usually go to see.

■ Ask an old friend out for tea.

■ Return to one favourite place from your childhood.

■ Paint a picture.

■ Buy and look after a pet.

■ Fall in love.

■ Spend some time in a toyshop (without a child with you).

■ Find at least three ways of making shopping more fun.

■ Pamper yourself with a trip to the hairdresser, aromatherapist, masseur, floatation tank, manicurist, reflexologist, chiropodist.

■ Write a letter to an old friend.

■ Buy a sex manual and read it (and use it).

■ Bake a cake or bread.

- Visit a wildlife sanctuary.
- Plan next year's holiday.
- Go on a train journey for fun.
- Do some charity work.

Summary

1 Make sure you are getting enough sleep and that your sleep patterns are regular.
2 If you suffer from continuous tiredness try some of the techniques recommended in this chapter.
3 Make sure you manage your time effectively.
4 Deal with difficult people in an appropriate manner.
5 Try to deal effectively with constant pain.
6 If you or your partner suffer from PMS then take positive action to relieve the symptoms.
7 Make sure you are kind to yourself and treat yourself occasionally.

7 | EMOTIONAL RELAXATION

According to Dr Thomas Stuttaford, gaining weight is not necessarily unhealthy; it depends where you put the weight on. Putting it on evenly over the body is much less unhealthy than putting it on unevenly. People who develop a bulky chest and abdomen while their limbs remain skinny are especially at risk of developing heart disease and diabetes. He says: 'The risk becomes much more apparent once the abdominal girth exceeds the hip measurement.' He advises men to make sure their waist measurements remain under 37 inches [94 cm] and women keep theirs under 31.5 inches [80 cm].

Many factors can affect our emotional relaxation and in this chapter we will look at some of them including depression, low self-esteem, expressing your feelings, partnerships and relationships, sex, parenthood and mid-life changes.

To have good emotional health we have to work hard to maintain balance in our lives. We have to be practical and acquire skills and resources we may never have thought necessary. With the pressure of modern living so intense it makes sense to seek support wherever we can.

Depression

We all get depressed from time to time. Some people seem to 'snap' out of it quickly and easily, but for others it can get a hold and lead to a downward spiral of feeling worse and worse. There are various factors which affect how quickly we can recover from bouts of depression as well as various factors which influence why we get depressed in the first place. They may well be linked. We may get depressed for any one of the following reasons.

- **Poor self-esteem**. If our view of ourselves is not what it might be – and this may well be caused by the way we were brought up – then we can feel intensely negative about ourselves. This can lead to unhappiness and a feeling that we are not worth bothering with.

- **Unexpressed emotions**. If we feel unable to express ourselves emotionally it can lead to us bottling up our feelings and the ensuing frustration can lead to depression.

- **Taking on too much**. Simply having too much to do, with too many demands being made upon our time and resources, can lead to depression especially if we feel we can't cope.

- **Illness**. Recovering from certain debilitating illnesses such as ME or glandular fever can be slow and can give rise to frustration and depression.

- **Brain chemicals**. We may have a deficiency of certain brain chemicals such as *noradrenalin* and *serotonin*. This shortage can affect depression levels. See a qualified medical practitioner if you think this is the case.

- **Hormonal**. Certain conditions such as *post-natal depression* can be brought about by a change in the body's hormone levels. This may be a temporary change in which case it will eventually revert to normal or, more long term which, if left unattended, can only get worse. In this case seek professional medical advice.

- **Grief**. If we have lost someone who was close to us through death or divorce or separation and we are not coping or dealing with our grief effectively it can lead to depression.

- **Patterns**. It is easy to get into a pattern of depression when faced with a problem because it is easier to succumb than to deal with the root causes.

- **Too high goals**. If we set our goals too high or make them too unrealistic then we are setting ourselves up for failure and this can be depressing if it happens continually.

Symptoms of depression

There may be times when we are depressed and not even realise it. We should know and be able to recognise the symptoms of depression not only in ourselves but in others. The symptoms are:

- sudden changes in levels of activity from active to apathetic and listless
- lack of interest in the outside world
- poor social contact
- loss of appetite
- loss of interest in sex
- poor sleep patterns
- inexplicable exhaustion and tiredness
- low self-confidence
- inability to make decisions
- lack of ability to concentrate
- sudden bouts of crying
- low self-esteem
- pessimism
- feelings of helplessness, guilt, irritability
- inability to take pleasure in anything.

Obviously having some of these symptoms doesn't necessarily mean that you are depressed – but they can be an early warning sign.

What can you do about depression?

Obviously prevention is better than cure – and some of the preventive techniques also work during bouts of depression and may help stave off the next attack.

- **Set goals**. Take control of your life and set yourself goals and make plans. If you drift aimlessly this will lead to feelings of helplessness. Having goals gives us motivation and ambition.
- **Be realistic about your goals**. Don't set goals that are too high or too difficult to achieve. Be realistic. Build in a failure factor so that when you do less well than intended it won't lead to feelings of inadequacy.
- **Step by step**. Don't take on too much. If you are depressed don't expect to make an instant recovery. Set yourself small tasks each day and feel pleased with yourself when you have accomplished them. Build up your reserves and strength again slowly. Be patient with yourself and expect setbacks.

■ **Write it all down**. Keep a diary. Write down each day how
  you feel and what you have done. If you keep a record you
  can see your improvement over a period of time which
  might otherwise go unnoticed.

■ **Express yourself**. Talk to friends and family. You are not
  alone. They may also feel like you do. It is good to get
  things off your chest.

■ **Be positive**. Don't allow negative thoughts. Be aware of
  'black and white' thinking – *it's all my fault, no one loves
  me, I won't get better, I'm a failure.* Think about what you
  are thinking.

■ **Get physical**. One of the quickest ways out of depression
  is to exercise. This releases natural antidepressant hormones called *endorphins*. If you are unfit you can try light
  gardening, walking, swimming or yoga.

Low self-esteem

If low self-esteem is the cause of emotional relaxation problems there are
ways of improving it. The following techniques can be tried but don't
expect instant results. Low self-esteem is invariably the result of many
years of negative programming and it takes a while to overcome it. Take
things slowly at first and build up your self-confidence step by step.

■ **Tomorrow is Day 1**. Learn from past mistakes but don't
  blame yourself for them. Begin each day as Day 1 and start
  again.

■ **Watch your body language**. If you are hunched and
  slumped you will feel low. This is also true in reverse. If
  you hold your head up and shoulders back you will feel
  happier. This is because your body posture affects your
  breathing. If you are slumped you are probably using
  upper-chest breathing. Sitting up and back makes you use
  diaphragmic breathing which makes you feel better.

■ **Dress the part**. Confident people wear confident clothing.
  They have neat, well-groomed hair. Follow their example.
  If you dress scruffily and don't take care of your personal
  hygiene and appearance you will feel less confident.

- **Rehearse the part**. Practise in front of a mirror. Stand up straight and look confident. See what your body does. Practise speaking in a confident way until it becomes easier to do it for real.
- **Avoid friends who drain you**. Socialise with high-energy friends. Stay away from anyone who reinforces your negative view of yourself. Hang out with people who praise you and make you feel good.
- **Be nice to yourself**. Treat yourself. Even in your worst moments be aware that you are still a valuable, unique, wonderful human being with special talents and skills and you need to be rewarded. If no one else does it, do it for yourself.
- **Be assertive**. What you want is important. Learn to approve of your needs and expect them to be met.
- **Plan your strategy**. Rehearse first. Plan how you will conquer a small fear and then go and do it. Visualise how the triumph will feel and then go and achieve it.
- **Don't be afraid to use others**. That's what they're there for. Express your feelings. Talk to people about how they can help you feel better. Value your importance and be prepared to tell others.

Expressing yourself

Telling people how you feel can be a big step towards leading a more relaxing and rewarding life. Research has shown that the more we bottle up our feelings the worse are the effects on our health. By learning to express ourselves we are helping ourselves become healthier, happier people. The more we do it, the more others will be encouraged to do it as well. Also the more we express, the less we bottle up to be released unintentionally later. For instance, if someone close to you dies, you would naturally be feeling extremely emotional and upset; but if your train was delayed by five minutes you might be only mildly annoyed. If you failed to express your grief at the right time you may find that it could spill over into an irrational rage on the station platform later.

■ **Monitor your feelings**. You can't express feelings if you don't know what you are feeling. Learn to tune into your body and how it affects your feelings and vice versa. What happens to your stomach when you feel nervous? What happens to your breathing when you feel angry? What happens to your body posture when you feel sad? Get to know what is happening. Ask yourself during the day 'How am I feeling right now?' Learn to watch your feelings as if they were happening to someone else; be objective about them; be realistic about them.

■ **It's good to talk**. Be honest with others about how you feel. Don't talk in clichés or platitudes about feelings. Open up and say how you really feel rather than just saying 'fine'. Watch what words you use when talking about your feelings. Don't be dramatic or extreme; be honest and realistic.

■ **Get physical**. If you have to shake someone's hand then do so with enthusiasm. If you have to hug someone do so with gusto. Stamp your feet if you're annoyed – it can work wonders. Be physically expressive. Touch people. Hold your partner's hand, cuddle, hug, touch your partner's face lovingly. Allow yourself to cry occasionally – it does you good. If you watch a sad film or read a sad novel then express your sadness and cry. If you want to smile at someone give them a radiant, beaming smile; laugh with others; sing out loud; shout with joy when you are happy.

Being sad

Sometimes when misfortune and tragedy come into our lives we need to be sad. If we lose a close friend or relative we need to grieve. If we get divorced or separated we need to come to terms with our loss and express our sadness.

■ **Accept nature**. All things go in cycles – life and death, beginnings and endings. If we accept that things change and there are cycles to life we can accept our loss more easily. It may not be what we want, but it is what must be.

■ **Time heals**. It can take up to three years to grieve properly for someone really close, but you will heal. Take it one day at a time.

- **Look after yourself**. You need proper sleep, food, rest and time to get over your loss – now more so than ever. Don't neglect yourself.
- **Get support**. If you are sad or grieving then say so and ask for help and support. Seek out professional help – it's what they are there for.
- **Talk about it**. Express how you feel. Don't bottle it up. Don't think that others don't want to be burdened. What you feel is valid and genuine. If you feel angry then express it. Don't feel guilty if your feelings seem inappropriate – they're not. They're yours and they're important.
- **Let it out**. If you need to cry or rage then do so. If you want time and space ask for it. If you feel the need to express your grief or sadness then it is important that you let it all out. You need to recognise your pain and experience the emotions to be able to come to terms with them, deal with them and get on with your life.
- **Move on**. You still have to live. Moving on doesn't mean forgetting or being heartless – it means you accept your loss (you may not like it or want it) and are ready to pick up the pieces of your life.

Relationships

One of the biggest areas for finding stress in our lives is within relationships, especially with our partner. Although we are supposed to be living in close, loving harmony things can go wrong and it is easy to build up resentments and frustrations by not being able to talk openly and honestly. How can we be relaxed when the hub of our life is not right? Working on our relationship is both rewarding, healthy and ultimately worthwhile because it gives us a stable base from which we can go out and explore the world. If it's wrong at home it will be wrong outside as well.

Swapping partners

A lot of people make the mistake of thinking that swapping their partner will bring them instant happiness and relief, only to find themselves back in the same stressful scenario within a short period of time. It's not the partner who needs changing nor the nature of relationships but rather ourselves and how we function in them. By starting with ourselves we can also help our partner improve the relationship with us.

RELATIONSHIPS QUESTIONNAIRE

Work through this checklist for yourself and see how you get on. There are no scores (and no prizes either) and only you can know if you answer the questions honestly. Your partner may like to try this action plan too, but don't put your partner under any pressure.

1 Do you *like* your partner?

2 Does your partner make you laugh?

3 If you weren't lovers would you be friends?

4 Do you respect your partner?

5 Are you sexually attracted to your partner?

6 Can you express your feelings to your partner openly and honestly?

7 Can your partner express feelings to you openly and honestly?

8 Do you enjoy any shared interests?

9 Who decides the major issues within the relationship?

10 Do you see your relationship continuing long term?

The questionnaire above may throw some new light on your relationship. You may find you need to resolve certain issues. The following are a few areas that can cause conflict and may need some attention.

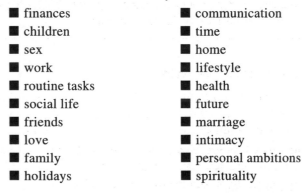

- finances
- children
- sex
- work
- routine tasks
- social life
- friends
- love
- family
- holidays
- communication
- time
- home
- lifestyle
- health
- future
- marriage
- intimacy
- personal ambitions
- spirituality

Obviously under each of these headings there will be many subheadings. For instance, suppose you feel that your finances together may need some work. You could come up with a list such as:

- joint accounts
- bills, housekeeping and mortgage
- spending money
- budgets
- savings and investments
- personal money
- overdrafts, loans and debts

You may need to sit down and go through all these areas with your partner until you are both happy with the situation. Remember that compromise is acceptable. You can also try the following action plan.

ACTION PLAN

1 Draw up a list of all the things you like, admire and enjoy about your partner.

2 Draw up a list of all the things that your partner does that annoy, irritate or make you angry. Write down any suggestions you might think of whereby you could change your response or change your partner's behaviour without changing basic personality. Remember that you dislike what your partner does – not your partner.

3 Make a list of all the things *you* do that irritate, annoy or make your partner angry. How could you change your behaviour? How might your partner change his or her response?

Increasing our success rate

There do seem to be some factors which indicate an increased success rate for a happy relationship – this doesn't mean that if you and your partner don't have any of these factors that you are doomed. The factors are:

- some shared interests and/or a similar background of upbringing, education, class and culture
- being physically/sexually attracted to each other

- having the same ideals and goals – especially long-term ones
- having opposite personalities – for instance, if you are shy and your partner is outgoing; or if you are boisterous and your partner is quieter; or if you are creative but unreliable whereas your partner is steadier and more reliable but not so dynamic.

Improving relationships

Here are some techniques you and your partner might like to try to improve your relationship.

- **You are allowed to talk**. Either of you can ask for time to talk. You may have to 'make an appointment' but neither can deny the other the right to talk if there is something you need to get off your chest. This isn't a session to moan about the other's behaviour but a genuine attempt to communicate. Allow about half an hour when you won't be disturbed by children or family or friends, and be open and honestly say what you need to say without the other interrupting. It is not necessary to reply afterwards – this is for the one who asked, having the time to express something important.

- **Draw up contracts**. If one of you persistently does something that irritates the other and the other wants the perpetrator to stop, ask for a contract to be drawn up where the other promises to stop. Include penalties if necessary. For instance, *'I promise to stop smoking in the bath. If I don't I will do the washing up for a week'*. Alternatively, you could plea bargain – *'I'll stop leaving the towels on the floor and you'll stop leaving the knife in the jam pot.'*

- **Be friends**. Sometimes we treat our partner in ways we wouldn't treat our friends. Endeavour to be as nice to each other as you would be to your friends.

- **Be surprising**. Try to surprise each other by breaking your routines or habits so that you don't become predictable and staid.

- **Be generous**. Treat each other occasionally to meals out, flowers, breakfast in bed, a massage with oils, a lie-in, a little gift, cooking a special meal.

■ **Spend time together**. Not just doing chores, bringing up the children or watching television, but real quality time together. Go for a walk and hold hands. Book a weekend in a hotel in Paris together. Special time together shouldn't be spent 'doing things' – just being together.

■ **Appreciate each other**. You both have a role and a function but that doesn't mean you should go unappreciated. Praise each other for the little tasks you take for granted. Be courteous with each other and say 'please' and 'thank you' and 'I appreciated it when you did ...' and 'it was really nice of you to ....'

■ **Reaffirm why you are together**. Make time to talk about how you met, how you fell in love, why you are together, where you are going together, how you feel about each other, what makes you feel good about the other person. Be positive.

Divorce and separation

If, however, you realise that you are with the wrong person and you have to separate there are ways to help you through this, also.

■ **Understanding what went wrong**. You are both in the relationship 50/50 and it is impossible to apportion blame. You must both share the responsibility no matter what went wrong. Even if you feel betrayed, cheated on, misled, lied to, deceived and abandoned. Remember that you chose, loved and trusted this person – no one made you. You had control and choice: you had a 50 per cent input. Even if a relationship ends badly there are no victims – you were both involved and at separation or divorce you are now both not involved. There is no blame.

■ **It isn't only you**. This is an experience many people have been through before – and are going through – and they all survive. Some even do better afterwards than they would ever have thought possible. Sometimes we cling to something worn out when we know we should be moving on and the pain of divorce or separation can sometimes kick-start us into a better, more rewarding life. You are not alone and others can guide and counsel you through this – they've been there before.

- **Don't take it personally**. Just because your partner and you have split up it doesn't devalue you as a person. Your friends and family still love and need you. You still have an important function in life, and there will be others.
- **Allow time to grieve**. If you are upset by separation and divorce treat it the same as you would a bereavement and allow time to grieve properly. Don't make any rash or hasty decisions now but wait until you have recovered.
- **Be nice to yourself**. Pamper yourself and treat yourself to something you've always wanted. Keep up your proper diet, sleep patterns and exercise. Don't let yourself go. Get out and make new friends, take up new interests and start new projects.
- **Relax**. Make sure you breathe properly and don't hyper-ventilate through tension. Study the plan for reducing panic attacks in Chapter 3. Make sure you keep practising any relaxation techniques that you know work for you.
- **Keep busy**. Fill in the time you used to spend on your relationship by embarking on a course of study, a new project, redecorating your entire home, travel – and if you feel up to it, a new relationship.

Sex

Sex is supposed to be one of the most relaxing activities we can enjoy but often becomes fraught with tension and difficulties. Most of these can be eliminated by a more open and honest expression of feelings and ideas. Here are some tips to help make sex more relaxing again.

- **It's good to talk**. Express your wants and needs, Encourage your partner to open up and explore wants and needs as well.
- **It's good to choose**. Make sure that you are enjoying sex within a committed and loving relationship where you can be open and honest. Choose a partner who makes you feel safe and wanted. Mutual respect is important.
- **It's good to experiment**. Encourage yourself and your partner to try new things, new places and new ways to

make love. Sex is an enormous subject and our wants and
needs change over time. Don't get stuck in a rut.

■ **It's good to give.** Lovemaking is just as much about giving
as it is about receiving. Don't be selfish. Make sure your
partner gets as much enjoyment and pleasure as you do.

■ **It's good to be open.** If you are shy or inhibited sexually
you can't enjoy it as much. Try to overcome the shyness
and explore in a safe atmosphere why you feel inhibited.
Work on your view of sex and try not to have too many pre-
conceived notions of what is 'right' or 'wrong'. Whatever
two people want to do together in a safe way is fine.

■ **It's good to know.** You cannot have good sex if you are
ignorant of any aspects of either your sexuality or your
partner's. You need to know how both men's and women's
bodies function sexually. You need to know what turns you
on and how to please your partner.

■ **It's good to do.** Sex is an important part of all of our lives
and we might need to make more time for it. Set aside some
special time for sex to which you can both look forward if
you need to, but make sure it is a regular part of your life.

■ **It's good to be intimate.** Sometimes one or either of you
will not feel like sex and the other should make allowances
for that. Our sexual appetite isn't static and there will be
times when we have less libido. You and your partner can
still caress, touch, stroke, massage and be close to each
other during these times. No sex doesn't mean no physical
contact.

Parenthood

Becoming a parent is something that will happen to many of us at some
time or another in our life. Perhaps it is unexpected and perhaps it is
planned – but however it happens we need to be both prepared and
skilled. Parenting is something you *can* make up as you go along but that,
as we have already seen in so many other areas, causes stress. It is better
to have as much information as possible, to research the subject and to
seek support and help from both family and professionals.

When you have a new baby in the home, especially if it is the first time, it can be very stressful. That applies to both parents; parenting is a joint venture and needs joint policies and decisions and support. You both contribute to the making of the baby and you both need to contribute to its upbringing. This makes sense for both yourselves and the baby. The more you put into your baby's development the more both emotionally and educationally you get out – and the better your baby develops.

Having a baby is one of the most, if not *the* most, stressful events that can occur in a relationship and you both need to work hard at it and be supportive and understanding.

Here are a few tips to help you through having a baby and out the other side, after about 20 years, more relaxed and sane.

- **Be together**. If one of you is pulling in a different direction it makes it much harder to cope. You will have little time for each other, but you have to make time. Plan evenings out together; get in babysitters right from the start so you maintain your relationship; have a set bedtime for the baby by the time it is few months old; spend time together without the baby so you can relax and remember why you got together in the first place; take time to reassure each other that you are still lovers/partners/friends; be nice to each other; support each other; look after each other.

- **Clear thinking**. Be aware of the *shoulds* and *musts*. There aren't any. How you bring up your baby together is up to you both. Try to change *should* to *want to*. For instance, instead of saying to yourself *'I should help her with the feeds'*, try saying to yourself *'I want to help her with the feeds'*; or instead of *'I should cook a supper for him'*, try *'I want to cook a supper for him'*. This may seem simplistic but it is surprisingly effective – it gets you questioning your thinking patterns and changing your responses.

- **Talk about it**. Having a baby, becoming a parent, generates a lot of feelings. We need to talk about them, express them. Some of them may not seem pleasant or exciting – frustration, jealousy, resentments and even anger – but when they are voiced they become less threatening. If we talk about them our partner has a chance to help, to relieve the stress symptoms before they overwhelm us. Give your partner time and space to talk openly and honestly about feelings. Listen without judgement and criticisms. Your partner is not talking about you and how your partner feels about you but about how your partner feels inside. Your partner's feelings, like yours, are valid and important.

■ **Support.** Don't be afraid to ask for whatever support is needed or available. Use friends, family, professionals and even neighbours to relieve the pressure. Most people are more than happy to look after a small child that isn't their own, even if it's for only a few minutes, to give you a break. Join a parent and baby group to share common experiences with other parents going through the same process as you. Use whatever professional support is available – if you have fears, doubts, worries ask your doctor, talk to your health visitor, go to the baby clinics, read books on the subject – but get help. If you can afford it, pay someone to come in once a week to help with the cleaning, or you may want to pay someone to be a full-time nanny.

■ **Be organised**. Work out a baby-duties rota for you and your partner so you both take turns looking after the baby and both have time off. Make sure you have an organised, safe, labour-saving environment to work in with the baby – easy-to-clean surfaces for changing nappies, as many disposable items as you can afford (bottles, nappies, etc.). Make life easier for you both by being efficient. For instance, don't make up only one bottle feed at a time – make up several, enough to last a day and keep some in the fridge.

■ **Have a life**. Spend time *not* talking about the baby. Keep up your outside leisure interests. Make sure you get some time off regularly to go out without the baby. Don't neglect your appearance. Keep to a healthy diet. Exercise regularly. Get as much sleep as possible. Do your relaxation exercises.

■ **Change your life**. You can't expect your life to be the same as it was before the baby arrived. Change your needs to be in line with the baby's. Sleep when the baby sleeps – this might mean taking an extra nap whenever the baby takes one. Just because things change it doesn't have to mean they are changing for the worse – have fun being a parent; don't take it all seriously. Make a game out of it.

■ **Nothing lasts**. Whatever stress and tension you are going through with a baby at any stage won't last. The sleepless nights are only a temporary thing. The vomiting all over your best jacket is only a temporary thing. Temper tantrums and the 'terrible twos' are only temporary things. It's fair to say that each stressful stage is superseded by another, even more stressful and dramatic. When things look bleak reassure yourself with the thought that 'this will pass', and indeed it will. The baby stage is only a temporary thing and we need to look forward to the end of each stressful phase and also to enjoy such moments – children are babies for such a short time; soon they become teenagers; and then they have left home – it all goes so quickly.

Mid-life changes

We all go through it – that time when we re-evaluate our life and probably find it wanting; then we expect instant and dramatic change. That change can be startling for others around us and emotionally it can threaten to overwhelm us. The feelings we have in our mid-life, usually around our early to mid forties, can be intense and we can feel so insecure and frightened by them that we over-react. Here are some tips to help you through this phase in a positive and dignified manner.

■ **You are not alone**. Others have gone before you and survived. Seek support from wherever necessary. Have therapy, talk to friends, talk to your doctor, talk (especially) to your partner. Read about the mid-life crisis. Gather as much information in advance as you can – be prepared.

■ **Put something back**. In middle age we question the value of our life. One way to restore our self-esteem is to put something back. Usually we have concentrated so much on ourselves – work, career, family – that we have neglected the larger world. To put something back, we can do some charity work, pass on our experience to others who are younger, become involved in local politics, become involved in a pressure group that interests us, take up new interests that will help others, or devote some time to those less fortunate than ourselves.

■ **Have a goal**. Plan your future. Set goals for yourself. Look ahead with interest and enthusiasm – it ain't over yet. Don't be negative in your thinking; there's still time to change careers, move abroad, start a family, write that book, create a garden, study a new subject, learn another language, take up a sport, get fit, lose weight, or learn to play a musical instrument.

■ **Feel young**. Nothing makes us feel older than our mental attitude. Take care of your appearance. Look after your physical needs. Don't neglect your health. Stay interested in the outside world. Keep abreast of fashions, politics, music, art, current thinking, modern technology. Don't let life slip past you.

■ **Seize the day**. Nature doesn't provide a mid-life crisis for nothing. This may be a good time to change, to re-evaluate, to take stock, and if you don't like what you see – then change it, but do it gently. Don't confront or threaten those close to you with new ideas all of a sudden. Be considerate. You may be feeling new emotions and it may be best to talk about them gradually and honestly – but do talk about them.

Achieving emotional relaxation

By now a pattern may be emerging of how you can relax and improve your emotional life. Basically, whatever situation you find yourself in emotionally, the techniques and advice don't change. Here is a summary of the top six tips for a more relaxed emotional life.

1 Be kind to yourself – pamper and treat yourself.
2 Look after yourself – diet, sleep, exercise.
3 Ask for help and support – both from friends and professionals.
4 Know as much about the situation as you possibly can so you are prepared.

5 Accept that things go in cycles and that there is a natural order to life.

6 Carry out relaxation techniques to encourage good breathing.

Square one philosophy

This is a relaxation technique to help you re-evaluate you life and see it as more positive. Imagine your life as a chess board. When you are born you enter at square one. As your life progresses you move across the squares. As each disaster strikes you have to move back one square. For instance, having a roof over your head moves you forward a square, as does having someone to love you, having someone you can love, having enough money, having good health, having a job, being fit, having a family. Any disaster moves you back a square; getting divorced moves you back one square, so does losing your job. You can consider yourself a failure or of no use whatsoever if you ever go all the way back to square one; then you really would have to start again. But you won't.

Building squares

The squares conquered always grow faster than the squares lost; this is another way of counting your blessings. Suppose you wake up in the morning and look out of the window to find your car has leaked all its brake fluid over the road – back a square. You manage to get it to the garage and they say it's going to cost a small fortune to repair – back a square. You get home and your partner tells you he or she loves you – forward a square. The cat's been sick over your briefcase – back a square. The dog looks up at you with such affection that you have to pat her – forward a square. Your favourite programme is on the television – forward a square. It's just been cancelled in favour of highlights of the sumo wrestling championships – back a square. Your partner offers to take you to the theatre and buy you a slap-up meal afterwards – forward a square. You get home and make mad, passionate love on the stairs – forward a square. You sleep soundly – forward a square. You wake up and remember you have no car to get you to work – back a square. However, at no point did you go back to square one. Each time disaster strikes just say to yourself *'Well, at least I'm not back at square one'*.

Summary

1 Do you suffer from depression? What can you do about it? What are some of the causes of depression?

2 How would you increase your low self-esteem if you were to suffer from it?

3 Can you express yourself clearly, honestly and well? What would you do about it if you couldn't?

4 What can you do to overcome sadness?

5 How can you monitor and improve your relationships? How can you improve your chances of a successful relationship?

6 How can you go about making the pain of divorce and separation better? What advice would you give to someone else going through such an event?

7 How can you improve your sex life?

8 What are the top six tips for emotional relaxation?

8 | STRESS AT WORK

Job dissatisfaction is bad for your health, according to Professor Cary Cooper of the University of Manchester Institute of Science and Technology. His study claims that 30 million working days are lost each year through stress. Dr James Lefanu agreed; male patients who answered negatively to enquiries about work were often found to be suffering from headaches, palpitations or sleeping difficulties. 'This distress poses a much more significant threat to the physical and mental wellbeing of young men than virtually everything else combined,' he says.

Before we can deal with stress at work and give suitable guidelines for relaxation we have to be able to identify the sources of the stress. To identify your sources of stress, fill in the following questionnaire. This questionnaire is used by occupational stress-management consultants and it has been found to be most beneficial in accurately pinpointing problem areas at work.

Tick the appropriate box for each question and make a note of the score.				
	Stress free 0	Low stress 1	Medium stress 2	High stress 3
1 Not enough work to do				
2 Too much work to do				
3 Responsibility for others and the way they work				
4 Workplace politics				
5 Changes in work patterns				

6	Too many different roles				
7	Work colleagues				
8	Close friends at work				
9	Remuneration				
10	Environment				
11	Overtime				
12	Taking work home				
13	Working hours – too long or unsociable				
14	Being uncertain as to what is required				
15	Having to make decisions				
16	Deadlines				
17	Boredom				
18	Fear of being dismissed				
19	Training				
20	Skills under utilised				
21	My relationship with my direct boss				
22	Thinking about work while away from it				
23	No clear goals to work towards				
24	Conflict at work				
25	Approval, praise and thanks				
26	Job satisfaction				
27	Being promoted too fast/too high				
28	Giving presentations and speaking at meetings				
29	Being closely supervised				
30	Promotion prospects				
31	Support from my partner				

32 Conflict with home life				
33 Outside interests conflicting with work				
34 No regular assessments				
35 Outside factors affecting work such as illness or finances				
36 Morale of work colleagues				

Each of these questions fits into one of six categories:

1 Home and work
2 Job satisfaction
3 Position
4 Responsibility
5 Working pressure
6 Work relationships

1 Home and work

[Add together your stress scores for questions 12, 22, 31, 32, 33, 35.]

For a stress score of over 12 for these six questions you should be thinking more about separating work from your home life. There should be firm boundaries between the two.

For a score of between 8 and 12 you are showing some signs of stress and need to look a little more closely at this issue.

For a score of under 8 you seem to be managing successfully to keep the two apart.

2 Job satisfaction

[Add together your stress scores for questions 9, 10, 18, 20, 26, 30.]

A score higher than 12 indicates low job satisfaction. You need to look at how highly praised and valued you are, and if not highly enough you need to question whether you are in the right job or working to the right levels of satisfaction.

For a score of between 8 and 12 you could do with being more satisfied and need to look at this area.

For a score of under 8 you seem to be enjoying work.

3 Position

[Add together your stress scores for questions 5, 6, 14, 17, 23, 34.]

For a score higher than 12 you need to clear up any misunderstandings about your role. What does you job description say? Reaffirm your position with your immediate boss and keep it clearly defined.

For a score of between 8 and 12 you still need to be clearer about your position.

For a score of under 8 you have obviously defined your position well and are happy with it.

4 Responsibility

[Add together your stress scores for questions 3, 4, 15, 24, 28, 29.]

For a score higher than 12 you seem to be stressed by the level of responsibilities you have. Perhaps too much is expected of you or you hold a post that you are not ready for yet or are unqualified to hold. You should seek retraining or support from colleagues.

For a score of between 8 and 12 there are problems and you need to look closely at this area.

For a score of below 8 you appear to be happy with the level of responsibility you hold.

5 Working pressure

[Add together your stress scores for questions 1, 2, 11, 13, 16, 27.]

A score higher than 12 would indicate you simply have too much work to do. You need to look at delegating or shedding some of your work load.

For a score of between 8 and 12 you are still under too much strain and need to look at this area closely.

For a score of under 8 you obviously have enough to do unless you find question 1 a problem in which case you have too little to do and should seek an increase in your work load or another form of employment.

6 Work relationships

[Add together your stress scores for questions 7, 8, 19, 21, 25, 36.]

For a score higher than 12 there is obviously severe conflict at work and you need to get immediate support from senior staff to deal with this.

For a score of between 8 and 12 there is obvious tension and you need to look at this area closely.

For a score of under 8 you appear to get on well with your work colleagues and find your working environment happy and relatively stress free.

Eliminating stress from work

Once we have isolated our problem areas at work we can do something about them. Here are some tips to help you eliminate stress from your work and be more relaxed about it.

- **Be clear about what is work and what is not**. Separate your work from your home life. Don't take work home with you – and don't take your home problems to work with you.
- **You are entitled to support**. If you need to retrain, develop new skills, improve, get help or even just talk about work problems, then you should be able to enlist support from the senior staff above you.
- **Work to live, not the other way round**. When all is said and done it's only a job. It might be important to you but your health, happiness and welfare come first.
- **Take breaks**. You need to get away from work now and again. This might be every few hours, days, weeks or months, but no one should expect you to work without suitable and beneficial breaks.
- **Have a life**. Make sure you don't spend all your time working, thinking about work, talking about work. Have some friends who don't work in the same business. Have hobbies and social activities that take you away from your work areas.
- **Don't take on too much**. You aren't superhuman. If you have junior staff, use them. Delegate. Learn to say 'no' to too much work.

- **Have a fixed working day – and stick to it**. Go home when you are supposed to. If you say you're going to stop at a certain time make sure you do.

- **Eat sensibly**. You should gear your food intake to the type of work you have to do. If you are a manual worker you need more calories. If your important meetings are in the afternoon don't have a heavy alcoholic lunch. Go easy on the garlic. Don't binge on high-calorie snacks. Watch your intake of coffee and other drinks containing caffeine. If you must smoke, try to cut down. Be aware of your drinking habits and patterns, and moderate them.

- **Be assertive**. If you feel under stress, then say so. Express your feelings at work. Don't bottle things up. Be honest with people.

- **Be focused at work**. You are there to do a task, so do it. You are not there for the social life, the free pens, the company car or the fine view from the office window.

- **Be organised**. Plan your work load, your desk, your diary, your day. Don't put things off, do things when you are supposed to and don't delay tasks.

- **Be comfortable**. Make sure your office chair is right for you. Make sure your working environment is warm enough/cool enough. Have whatever you need to be comfortable enough to get the job done properly, but not so comfortable that you fall asleep.

- **Be safe**. Make sure you are working in an environment that is suitable. Check your Health and Safety regulations.

- **Be committed**. If you have chosen to do the job then get on with it. If you find you can't then change jobs.

- **Set goals**. Make sure the job you are doing furthers your personal life goals and that you aren't just filling in time waiting for something better to turn up. Make plans to make sure your job does further your goals if that is the case.

- **Be healthy**. Make sure the job is not detracting from your health. This applies to your moral and emotional health just as much as your physical health. If the job you are doing goes against the grain of your personal views and beliefs you will suffer stress.

But what if you are without work because you are either unemployed or retired? Both of these states have associated relaxation techniques to help you stay sane.

Unemployment

■ **Keep busy**. Don't allow time to hang on your hands. Keep active. You can use this time to acquire new skills, embark on a new course of study or improve what skills you already have. You can also use this time to keep physically fit by doing such exercise as walking, jogging, running, swimming or weight training, all of which are either free or relatively low cost.

■ **Be kind to yourself**. Look after yourself properly. Be positive and make sure you maintain personal hygiene and good grooming. Take care of your appearance. Make sure you treat yourself occasionally and go out as much as you can to meet friends and enjoy a social life.

■ **Be positive**. Make sure you plan your time properly and that you see getting a job as a definite project and a goal. You have to motivate yourself and do all the work yourself – it's a bit like being self-employed or freelance.

Retirement

■ **Be prepared**. If your retirement is coming up then make plans for it. You need to check that you can cope financially; that your partner is prepared for your change in working patterns; that you are emotionally prepared; that you have other interests; that you have things to fill your time that mean something to you.

■ **See it as a positive change**. Look forward to retirement as the opportunity to do all the things you haven't been able to do before. See it as freedom from, rather than not being wanted by, work. Take the opportunity to travel, study, start new projects, learn new skills, write, meet new people, take up new leisure interests, get fitter, take up a new sport.

■ **What can you give back?** Our working life is growing shorter as each new generation lives longer. As a percentage of our lives the work part is getting less. We need to be aware that what is left is still a considerable amount of time and it can be filled constructively by giving something back. What could you teach/show younger people? Your experience is still valid and worthwhile and you are still a respected and valued member of society. Retirement is not only an ending; it is also a major beginning and needs to be seen as such.

Summary

1 Identify where your stress comes from at work.
2 Complete the questionnaire and rate your work stress.
3 Work out what you have to do to eliminate stress from your work.
4 Check the guidelines for unemployment.
5 Check the guidelines for retirement.

9 | RELAXATION GOALS

Holidays can tear your family apart and ruin your happiness. A recent Barclaycard survey of 2,000 holidaymakers revealed that four in 10 family holidays result in bitter arguments between spouses. Half of all holidaymakers found the travelling 'very stressful', while 20 per cent said they felt ill while away, and 40 per cent reported they couldn't wait to get home.

Relate, formerly the Marriage Guidance Council, also reported a rise in demand for its services after the holiday season which 'could be linked to families spending unaccustomed time cooped up together'.

The answer, says psychologist Trevor Jellis, an adviser to Barclaycard, might be to avoid the traditional two-week break altogether. 'Shorter but more frequent breaks recharge the batteries just as well as longer holidays. Others might put their relationships under less strain by taking a complete break from each other.'

Long-term planning

You've got to have a plan. Without plans we are lost on a sea of randomness. Our plans may go wrong, fail to materialise, be substituted and amended. But we've got to make plans if we want to be relaxed about the future – it gives us a sense of control. One of the things that stops us from making plans is our sense of failure – so build that into your plans as well. Here are some tips for planning long-term goals.

■ **Identify the hurdles**. Knowing what can stop you from achieving your goals is a step towards overcoming the hurdles. Perhaps your finances, your personality or your family commitments are your potential hurdles. Once you have identified the hurdles you can see ways to overcome them – but you have to know them first.

- **Write it all down**. Draw up an action plan. Next to each item you can list what you need to achieve your goals and what you expect from them. You may need to learn new skills to achieve them so you can mark each item with a further action plan.

- **Brainstorm**. Ask your partner/close friends/family to help you. Write down anything/everything you can think of relating to your future goal. It doesn't matter how silly or preposterous anything is – write it down. You never know when something will be useful or spark you off on a different chain of thought that will lead you to a solution or idea.

- **Be realistic**. Don't make plans or attempt goals that you simply know you cannot achieve. Into every plan allow space for your own personality – we might be able to change a bit and improve but we cannot alter our basic personality. So if your plan expects you to be terribly fit and athletic and you are by nature sedentary and slothful – forget it.

- **Prioritise**. Check your plan for what is most important to you and make it top of your list.

- **No conflicts**. Make sure your plans and goals don't conflict with each other. For instance, you might plan to retire to a Greek island; you might also plan to spend your retirement painting watercolours of churches in the Cotswolds. This is an obvious conflict (yes, I know it's a silly example but it's the sort of thing I do).

- **Be clear**. What exactly do you want? Be clear about the detail of your plan. You might decide you want to paint. That's fine. But what sort of painting? Oils? Watercolours? What will you paint? Where? What sort of training do you need? Do you have an aptitude for it? What will you do with the finished pictures? Being clear means saying '*I want to paint watercolours of churches in the Cotswolds after I have done an evening class learning about watercolours. I intend to sell my paintings in local craft shops and display them in the local gallery.*' This naturally leads you on to:

■ **Research your plan**. Does the local craft shop sell many watercolour paintings by hopeful amateurs? Does the local gallery display such paintings? How much money do they sell for? What are the costs of your raw materials? All this may sound a lot of work but it enables you to fulfil your plans, cancel any that are unrealistic and be prepared. The more you know the more you can achieve.

■ **Reward yourself**. For each step of your plan, as it comes to fruition, you can reward yourself. Plan these rewards in advance. For instance, you could say *'When I sell those four paintings I will treat myself to a new easel.'* This will provide you with motivation as well as being kind to yourself.

■ **Know the results**. Be clear about what you think the results of your plans will be. For instance, if you plan to move to a Greek island what will that achieve apart from a good sun tan? Do you expect to be lonely? Meet new friends quickly? Be able to speak Greek within six months and then be accepted as a local? You could, for instance, say *'I am moving to a Greek island. This will enable me to get on with my painting; provide a holiday home for my grown-up children which means I will see more of them and my grandchildren; give me the opportunities to study Greek archaeology which I have always wanted to know more about; enable me to be fitter and more healthy, improve my diet and take up swimming again'*. Surely this is better than just *'I fancy moving to Greece'*?

■ **Be prepared to change plans**. Write an element of contingency for both change and failure into your plans. There will always be unexpected events and information which you can't know about when making your plans so you have to be flexible in your thinking. If you set your heart on something special and it fails to materialise you can suffer stress through disappointment. But if you are flexible you can swiftly change your plans to accommodate the unexpected. Suppose you planned to open an antique shop in a pretty village only to discover at the last minute that a bypass or motorway was about to be built straight through it. What could you do to be flexible? Change villages? Change shops? Maybe a transport café would be better? Only you can know what you would do but be flexible in your thinking.

Changing your thinking patterns and habits

In the set of tips above, the last one was about being flexible in your thinking. Here are some tips to help you achieve this.

- **Watch what you say**. Every time you use the words *should*; *have to*; *must*; *got to*; *ought to* stop and think – question why you *should?*; why do you *have to?*; who said you *must?*; why have you *got to?*; whose rule is it that you *ought to?*. This obviously also applies to the opposites – *shouldn't, can't, mustn't, oughtn't*. This rigid thinking causes us great stress without us even realising. We can benefit from questioning where we get all these rules and regulations from. Who decides what we should do, ought to do, must do, have to do? When it is us that's fine, but if we are living our lives according to somebody else's criteria we can never achieve true independence, control and happiness, and, of course, be relaxed.

- **Listen to what others say**. You know the five key phrases to listen out for. Who is telling you that you *should*; *have to*; *must*; *got to*; *ought to*? Why do they tell you what to do? What's in it for you? What's in it for them? Watch out for a finger being pointed at you and one of those five phrases being said to you. Learn to fire them back again. If someone tells you that you *must*; ask *'why must I?'* If they say you've *got to*; ask *'why have I got to?'* These five phrases are fine for children but as adults we really don't need them that much.

- **Know as much as you can**. Without sufficient information we simply can't make decisions or be flexible enough in our thinking. Ask questions – you may not like the answers but at least you'll know. Having information changes our thinking. The more we have the less fear, uncertainty and hesitation we suffer.

- **Watch your moods**. When we are tired, stressed or bad tempered our thinking becomes much more rigid. When we are relaxed, happy and rested our thinking is much more flexible and we are better able to make decisions, make plans and be realistic.

- **Be experienced**. We all have fears of the unknown. We believe we simply *can't* because we have never tried. When we have experience of things we are better able to cope. Only by knowing can we understand. We have to try – even if we fail – just to expand our horizons and add to our experience.

- **We are all the same**. Everyone around you suffers from rigid thinking just as much as you do – make allowances. Not everyone will have read this book so they may not be as relaxed about life as you are – make allowances.

Getting things done

So now you have sorted out your rigid thinking and made your plans you are ready to leap into the future – that is unless you keep putting it off. How do we avoid procrastination? Here are a few tips.

- **Set yourself deadlines**. Set a limit for when you expect to have achieved certain goals. Don't leave plans open-ended by saying, for instance, *'I will go to an evening class in basket making'*. Rather say *'I will enrol next Monday and start the class on the first Wednesday in September.'*

- **Go for it**. Dare yourself. Set yourself challenges – and then just go for it. Summon up your courage, don't allow yourself time to talk yourself out of it – just do it.

- **Know yourself**. Write down all the things you've been putting off. Write down next to them the list of excuses you make. Can you see the pattern? What is the problem? Is it the things that need doing – or is it you? Once we know the sort of excuses we habitually come up with, we can laugh at ourselves and get on with it.

- **Reward yourself**. Each time you complete a step in your plan reward yourself. This motivates you better than anything else.

- **Be realistic**. If your plan is too difficult you won't even begin to carry it out. Lower your expectations. Know your limits and don't push them too far beyond your capabilities.

- **Ask 'Why?'** Write a list of all the advantages of doing something – and all the disadvantages. Why are you putting it off? What can you gain by procrastination? What can you gain by getting on with it?

- **Bit by bit**. If the task or plan seems overwhelming take it a step at a time. Divide up tasks into manageable bits and reward yourself when you've done some of it – you are working towards a long-term goal and each step is a success in itself.

Accepting yourself

Once you start doing this sort of work you get to know yourself better. When you know yourself, you can see the patterns emerging and can take appropriate action. Here are a few tips for getting to know yourself even better – and when you really know yourself, you can relax, safe in the knowledge that you're doing OK.

- **Learn from your mistakes**. That's why you make them – they're not flaws in character or imperfections; they're learning tools. Each time you foul up you have a unique opportunity to improve, to grow and to learn.

- **Nobody's perfect**. Each part of your character is important – and that includes all the 'bad' bits. You are unique and wonderful, exactly as you are. If you choose to work on yourself and try to improve then that's your decision, but you are doing it out of choice not to impress others or to please others. By accepting you, as you are, you are more likely to be at peace and relaxed.

- **Don't fear failure**. By being afraid to make a mistake or to fail you run the risk of doing nothing. If you accept the challenge of failing and making mistakes you can achieve much because you aren't afraid. It doesn't matter if you fail – you can even see it as a positive benefit because then you can learn from it and move on.

- **Be honest**. If you have what you consider to be 'weaknesses' then let them show. Don't be afraid to admit you feel nervous or insecure or frightened. No one wants you to be perfect or superhuman. We all have fears and doubts and the best way to deal with them is to admit them – both to yourself and others. You may find you are not as alone or as unusual as you thought.

- **Set yourself goals**. Only by *trying* to improve and learn can we do so. You could try saying something like *'I know I'm useless at cooking so I'm going to do an evening class, starting the first Wednesday in September, and then I can surprise my friends by cooking a fabulous dinner for them all.'*

- **Be here now**. Don't live in the future or the past. Live here, now, in the present. Count your blessings and enjoy the moment. The future will be along in a moment without any help from you, and there is nothing you can do to alter the past. You could suggest to yourself that you have endured: *childhood, adolescence, growing up, employment, love, disappointments, fears, storms, floods, winters, disasters, accidents and all the stuff life can throw at you* – and for what? Why, to arrive at this moment, this now that we exist in. If you have gone through all that to arrive at this present then maybe you'd better get on and enjoy it because it's been such a struggle, such a long journey. It's taken you all of your life so far just to arrive at now.

Taking care of yourself

It's a long life and you need to carry out routine maintenance and servicing on the vehicle that will carry you through it. Here are the top tips for looking after yourself. They are not arranged in any particular order – they are all equally important.

- Give yourself lots of treats and rewards.
- Make time to relax.
- Be with people you like and who make you happy.
- Eat healthily.

- Be selfish when you need to be without guilt.
- Make sure your leisure activities please and satisfy you without needing to 'have a point' to them.
- Make plans that you can look forward to.
- Be assertive.
- Take responsibility for your own life.
- Let others take responsibility for their own lives.
- Take your time – there's no point rushing.
- Avoid things which hurt your body such as excessive alcohol, tobacco, drugs, danger and extremes of temperature.
- Constantly strive to improve your education and studying.
- Look after your appearance.
- Praise and approve of yourself.
- Exercise and keep fit.
- Enjoy pleasurable activities and do some every day.
- Sleep properly and regularly.
- Express your emotions and talk to people about them.
- Allow others to get close to you.
- Be kind to yourself when you let yourself down.
- Have a spiritual dimension to your life.
- Avoid hurting others wherever possible.

Don't worry – be happy

The more relaxed we are the less we worry – and the reverse is also true. The more we worry the less we can relax. Not worrying doesn't mean negating our responsibilities or neglecting our duties. Not worrying means identifying the problem and solving it. When we stop worrying we can relax and be soothed. Here are the top tips for reducing our worrying capacity.

- **Isolate the worry.** Sometimes we think we are worrying about a particular problem when it is actually something entirely different that is triggering our cause for concern. For instance, we might worry unduly about where our teenage children are at night and rationalise that they might be in danger or getting up to mischief. What we really want is for them to come home because then we can go to bed as we need a good night's sleep before an important meeting tomorrow ... and that meeting is what we are *really* worrying about.

■ **Be aware of the damage**. Know what harm you are doing to yourself by worrying. Do something about it now. The more you worry the less you can relax. The less you relax the more stress you carry. The more stress you carry the more your health is affected. The more your health is affected the less benefit you are to yourself and society. Be positive in your need to deal with worrying.

■ **Worst-case scenario**. Mentally map out the worst possible outcome, and know that whatever happens the worst case is unlikely to happen. It might, but it probably won't. Then you can relax at least a little bit knowing that your worst fears won't happen. Now think of the best-case scenario and know that the reality will fall somewhere in between the two. That's not so bad, is it? Suppose you've taken your car in for its annual test. Worst case – it fails and has to be scrapped. Best case – it passes with flying colours. True case – it needs a new set of brakes and costs you quite a bit, but at least you still have your car and don't have to walk everywhere.

■ **See beyond the worry**. Whatever it is that you are worry-ing about will pass. Let's suppose you are worrying about how to pay the telephone bill. Picture yourself in six months. The bill will have been paid and you'll probably be worrying about another one. Remember all the many hundreds of bills you've had in the past? You worried about them all – and where are they now? All paid, of course. How? You probably won't even remember, but paid they were – and all that worry was needless.

■ **Be realistic**. How much evidence do you have? Suppose you worry that your children are taking drugs. How much evidence do you have? Are they staying out all night? Are they associating with known drug addicts? Are they show-ing symptoms of drug addiction? Have you found evidence around the house of drug paraphernalia? Are you just worrying needlessly? Start worrying when you have solid evidence – or rather, don't start worrying – take action that is appropriate to the particular problem.

■ **Set aside time**. Schedule into your day half an hour when you can sit down and worry without interruption or guilt. When you find yourself trying to worry you probably won't be able to, but it's worth a try just to see how funny it might feel to worry to order.

■ **What can I do?** As soon as a new worry crops up ask yourself *'What can I do?'* Refuse to worry unless you identify positive action you can take. Worry about what you can change and let go of the rest. For instance, worrying about the world's hunger problems is pointless – there is simply nothing you can do on such a vast scale. Worrying about a friend who has fallen on hard times is worthwhile – you can do something – offer to lend your friend money, offer to help, invite your friend to express any concerns and problems, be there for your friend.

■ **Be a Supreme Being**. Whenever you have a worry imagine that it is not you who is worrying, imagine it is someone else. Now imagine that you are a Supreme Being – all knowing, all powerful. What advice would you give to the person who is worrying? What would you say? This may sound silly until you try it. When you see your worries from outside they will take on a different perspective. If you imagine it is someone else worrying you can be much more objective and rational in your advice. Try it.

■ **Listen to your mind**. Are you worrying in such terms as *should, got to, must, ought to, have to*? If your inner voice is using any of these terms give it a strict talking to and tell it to behave itself.

■ **Lighten up**. If you find yourself worrying ask yourself how important it is. How does your worry rate on a scale of 1 to 10? If you say that 1 is mildly worrying but completely trivial and unimportant, and 10 is a threat to the fabric of society, how does your worry score? If it's up around 9 or 10 then please feel free to worry (or re-examine your scoring process). If it's around 1 or 2 you've probably got something better to be getting on with. If it's in between then you need to stop worrying and take appropriate action to solve the problem.

■ **Keep busy**. You worry only when you have the time to do so. By keeping busy you distract yourself and simply can't worry. You can keep busy in all sorts of ways – buy a set of worry beads, sing loudly, move house, have a baby, go on holiday, change jobs, cook a meal, do a jigsaw, talk to friends, go shopping, learn a new skill, take up a hobby, go for a walk, take a bath, do a household chore, decorate your home, go to the cinema – do whatever it takes, but be busy if you are prone to worrying. Be happy.

APPENDIX: RELAXATION THERAPIES

Women suffering from clinical depression are at risk of suffering from broken bones according to a new American study. The link has been made by researchers at the National Institute of mental health in Maryland. A group of 24 women suffering from major depression, or with a history of it, was found to have a significantly lower bone density than a group of healthy women of the same age, size and weight. Dr David Michelson and his team believe this is due to increased secretion of a hormone, cortisol, a common feature of depression.

Acupressure

Acupressure is based on the same ancient Chinese principles as acupuncture, but instead of needles, finger pressure is used on specific body points. As with acupuncture, it is used to treat a variety of ailments, including relief from the pain of arthritis, menstrual cramps, muscle tension, and various other aches and pains. Acupressure is also used to improve overall health and wellbeing.

Acupuncture

Acupuncture originated in China more than 5,000 years ago. It is based on the belief that good health is determined by a balanced flow of *ch'i* (also referred to as *qi*), the life energy present in all living beings. According to acupuncture theory, ch'i circulates in the body along 12 major energy pathways, called *meridians*, each linked to specific internal organs and organ structures. There are over 1,000 *acupoints* within the meridian system that can be stimulated to enhance the flow of ch'i. When special needles are inserted into these acupoints (just under the skin), they help to correct and rebalance the flow of energy and consequently relieve pain and/or restore health.

Alexander Technique

The Alexander Technique stresses the importance of re-educating the muscular system as a means to achieve physical and mental wellbeing. Suffering from chronic voice loss, the actor F. Matthias Alexander developed this technique. Alexander teachers use hands-on guidance and verbal instruction to teach simple and efficient ways of relieving tension and stress by improving balance, posture and co-ordination.

Applied kinesiology (touch for health)

Applied kinesiology can determine health imbalances in the body's organs and glands by identifying weaknesses in specific muscles. By stimulating or relaxing these key muscles, an applied kinesiologist can diagnose and resolve a variety of health problems.

Aromatherapy

Aromatherapy is a unique branch of herbal medicine that uses the medicinal properties found in the essential oils of various plants. Through a process of steam distillation or cold-pressing, the volatile constituents of the plant's oil (its essence) are extracted from its flowers, leaves, branches, or roots. The oils exert much of their therapeutic effect through their pharmacological properties and their small molecular size, making them one of the few therapeutic agents to penetrate the bodily tissues easily.

Ayurvedic medicine

Practised in India for more than 5,000 years, Ayurvedic medicine (meaning 'science of life') is a comprehensive system of medicine that combines natural therapies with a highly personalised approach to the treatment of disease. Ayurvedic medicine places equal emphasis on body, mind and spirit, and strives to restore the harmony of the individual.

'Constitution' is the keystone of Ayurvedic medicine, and refers to the overall health profile of the individual, including strengths and susceptibilities. Once established, it becomes the foundation for all clinical decisions. According to the person's metabolic body type (constitution), a specific treatment plan is designed to guide the individual back into harmony with the environment. This may include dietary changes, exercise, yoga, meditation, massage, herbal tonics, herbal sweat baths, medicated enemas, and medicated inhalations.

Bach Flower Remedies

The emotions play a crucial role in the health of the physical body. Bach Flower Remedies directly address a person's emotional state in order to help facilitate both psychological and physiological wellbeing. By balancing negative feelings and stress, the Flower Remedies can effectively remove the emotional barriers to health and recovery.

Biofeedback training

Biofeedback training is a method of learning how to consciously regulate normally unconscious bodily functions (such as breathing, heart rate and blood pressure) in order to improve overall health. It refers to any process that measures and reports back immediate information about the biological system of the person being monitored so the person can learn to influence that system consciously. Biofeedback is particularly useful for learning to reduce stress, eliminate headaches, control asthmatic attacks, recondition injured muscles, and relieve pain.

Biological dentistry

Biological dentistry treats the teeth, jaw, and related structures with specific regard to how treatment will affect the entire body. Biological dentistry stresses the use of non-toxic restoration materials for dental work, and focuses on the unrecognised impact that dental toxins and hidden dental infections have on overall health.

Bodywork

The term bodywork refers to therapies such as massage, deep tissue manipulation, movement awareness and energy balancing, which are employed to improve the structure and functions of the human body. Bodywork in all its forms helps to reduce pain, soothe injured muscles, stimulate blood and lymphatic circulation, and promote deep relaxation.

Cell therapy

Cell therapy promotes physical regeneration through the injection of healthy cellular material into the body. It is used to stimulate healing, counteract the effects of ageing, and treat a variety of degenerative diseases, such as arthritis, Parkinson's disease, atherosclerosis and cancer. Although not approved in the United States, cell therapy is used throughout Europe and in many countries worldwide.

Chelation therapy

Chelation (pronounced key-lay-shun) comes from the Greek word *chelo* meaning 'to claw'. Chelation therapy is a safe and effective method for drawing toxins and metabolic wastes from the bloodstream. Chelating agents administered intravenously have been proven to increase blood flow and remove arterial plaque. Chelation therapy can help reverse atherosclerosis, can prevent heart attacks and strokes, and is used as an alternative to bypass surgery and angioplasty.

Chi Kung

Chi Kung (also known as *qigong*) is an ancient Chinese exercise that stimulates and balances the flow of ch'i, or vital life energy, along the acupuncture meridians (energy pathways). Like acupuncture and Traditional Chinese Medicine, the Chi Kung tradition emphasises the importance of teaching the patient how to remain well. In China, the various methods of Chi Kung form the nucleus of a national self-care system of health maintenance and personal development. Chi Kung cultivates inner strength, calms the mind, and restores the body to its natural state of health by maintaining the optimum functioning of the body's self-regulating systems.

Chiropractic

Chiropractic is concerned with the relationship of the spinal column and the musculoskeletal structures of the body to the nervous system. Proper alignment of the spinal column is essential for optimum health because the spinal column acts as the central switching organisation for the nervous system. When there is nerve interference caused by misalignments in the spine, known as *subluxations*, pain can occur and the body's defences can be diminished. By adjusting the spinal joints to remove subluxations, normal nerve function can be restored.

Colon therapy

The colon, along with the skin, kidneys and lungs, is a major organ for eliminating bodily waste. The healthy function of the colon is essential for good digestion and the proper absorption of nutrients. If bowel movements are not consistent, waste products and toxins are not eliminated in a proper manner, and ill health can occur. Colon therapy uses a series of colonic water flushes to clean and detoxify the lower intestine and aid in the reconstitution of intestinal flora.

Craniosacral therapy

Craniosacral therapy manipulates the bones of the skull to treat a range of conditions, from headache and ear infections to stroke, spinal cord injury and cerebral palsy. For decades various forms of cranial manipulation have been used to improve overall body functioning, and today Craniosacral therapy is gaining acceptance by health professionals worldwide as a successful treatment.

Detoxification therapy

Each year people are exposed to thousands of toxic chemicals and pollutants in the earth's atmosphere, water, food, and soil. These pollutants manifest themselves in a variety of symptoms, including decreased immune function, neurotoxicity, hormonal dysfunction, psychological disturbances and even cancer. Detoxification therapy combined with special cleansing diets or juice-and-water fasts help to rid the body of chemicals and pollutants and can facilitate a return to health.

Diet

A dietician will pay attention not only to what we eat but also to how it is grown or reared; what chemicals were used in its production; how it is stored and processed; how it is cooked and prepared; and even how it is served.

Energy medicine

Energy medicine uses diagnostic screening devices to measure the various electromagnetic frequencies emitted by the body in order to detect imbalances that may be causing present illness, or contributing to future disease. These disturbed energy flows can then be returned to their normal, healthy state through the input of electromagnetic signals that specifically counteract the affected frequencies to restore normal energy balance within the body.

Environmental medicine

Environmental medicine explores the role of dietary and environmental allergens in health and illness. Factors such as dust, moulds, chemicals and certain foods may cause allergic reactions that can dramatically influence diseases ranging from asthma and hay fever to headaches and depression. Virtually any chronic physical or mental illness may be improved by the care of a physician competent in this field.

Enzyme therapy

For every chemical reaction that occurs in the body, enzymes provide the stimulus. Enzymes are substances that make life possible, they help to build the body from proteins, carbohydrates, and fats. The body may have the raw building materials, but without the enzymes, it cannot begin.

Enzyme therapy can be an important first step in restoring health and wellbeing by helping to remedy digestive problems. Plant enzymes and pancreatic enzymes are used in complementary ways to improve digestion and absorption of essential nutrients. Treatment includes enzyme supplements, coupled with a healthy diet that features whole foods.

Fasting

Fasting is a low-cost, effective therapy for a wide range of conditions, including hypertension, headaches, allergies and arthritis. By relieving the body of the task of digesting foods, fasting allows the system to rid itself of toxins while facilitating healing. Fasting should be done only over short periods – never more than two days without medical supervision.

Guided visualisation

Visualisation is simply a flow of thoughts that one can see, hear, feel, smell or taste in one's imagination. Using the power of the mind to evoke a positive physical response, guided visualisation can reduce stress and slow heart rate, stimulate the immune system and reduce pain. As part of the rapidly emerging field of mind/body medicine, guided imagery is being used in various medical settings, and, when properly taught, can also serve as a highly effective form of self-cure.

Herbal medicine

The word herb as used in herbal medicine (also known as botanical medicine or, in Europe, as phytotherapy or phytomedicine), means a plant or plant part that is used to make medicine, food flavours (spices), or aromatic oils for soaps and fragrances. A herb can be a leaf, flower, stem, seed, root, fruit, bark, or any other plant part used for its medicinal, food-flavouring or fragrant property.

Herbs have provided humankind with medicine from the beginning of civilisation. Throughout history, various cultures have handed down their accumulated knowledge of the medicinal use of herbs to successive generations. This vast body of information serves as the basis for much of traditional medicine today.

Homoeopathy

The word homoeopathy derives from the Greek word *homoios*, meaning 'similar', and *pathos*, meaning 'suffering'. Homoeopathic remedies are generally dilutions of natural substances from plants, minerals and animals. Based on the principle of 'like cures like', these remedies specifically match different symptom patterns or 'profiles' of illness, and act to stimulate the body's natural healing response.

Hydrotherapy

Hydrotherapy is the use of water, ice, steam, and hot and cold temperatures to maintain and restore health. Treatments include full-body immersion, steam baths, saunas, hip baths, colonic irrigation and the application of hot and/or cold compresses. Hydrotherapy is effective for treating a wide range of conditions and can easily be used in the home as part of a self-care programme.

Hyperthermia

Fever is one of the body's most powerful defences against disease. Hyperthermia artificially induces fever in the patient who is unable to mount a natural fever response to infection, inflammation or other health challenges. It is used locally or over the entire body to treat diseases ranging from viral infections to cancer, and is an effective self-help treatment for the common cold and 'flu.

Hyperthermia takes advantage of the fact that many invading organisms tolerate a narrower temperature range than body tissues and are, therefore, more susceptible to increases in temperature. Hyperthermia treatments may not be able to kill every invading organism, but they can reduce their numbers to a level the immune system can handle. Hyperthermia stimulates the immune system by increasing the production of antibodies and interferon (a protein substance produced by virus-invaded cells that prevents reproduction of the virus). Hyperthermia is also a useful technique in detoxification therapy because it releases toxins stored in fat cells.

Hypnotherapy

For thousands of years the power of suggestion has played a major role in healing in cultures as varied as ancient Greece, Persia and India. Hypnotherapy uses both the power of suggestion and trance-like states to access the deepest levels of the mind to effect positive changes in a person's behaviour, and to treat a range of health conditions, including migraines, ulcers, respiratory conditions, tension headaches and even warts.

Juice therapy

Juice therapy follows a system of cleansing and restoration, and uses the fresh, raw juice of vegetables and fruits to nourish and replenish the body. Used as nutritional support during periods of stress and illness, juice therapy can also be used as part of a comprehensive health maintenance plan.

Light therapy

Many health disorders can be traced to problems with the circadian rhythm, the body's inner clock, and how it governs the timing of sleep, hormone production, body temperature and other biological functions. Disturbances in this rhythm can lead to health problems such as depression and sleep disorders. Natural sunlight and various forms of light therapy, including full-spectrum ultraviolet, coloured and laser light, can help re-establish the body's natural rhythm and are becoming an integral treatment for many related health conditions.

More recently, the ability of light to activate certain chemicals has become the basis of treatment for skin disorders such as psoriasis and for some forms of cancer. Exposure to ultraviolet light under controlled conditions has also proved beneficial for various conditions, particularly when combined with light-sensitive medications.

Magnetic field therapy

The world is surrounded by magnetic fields: some are generated by the earth's magnetism, while others are generated by solar storms and changes in the weather. Magnetic fields are also created by everyday electrical devices: motors, televisions, office equipment, computers, microwave ovens, the electrical wiring in homes, and the power lines that supply electricity to homes. Even the human body produces subtle magnetic fields that are generated by the chemical reactions within the cells and the ionic currents of the nervous system.

Recently, scientists have discovered that external magnetic fields can affect the body's functioning in both positive and negative ways, and this observation has led to the development of magnetic field therapy.

Massage

There are many different types of massage from passive and gentle to extremely deep and active. Massage can be used to help patients recovering from operations, to help sports people improve their efficiency, soothing pain, aiding relaxation, helping people back to general fitness, reducing strain to soft tissues, cleansing bodily tissues, improving circulation, easing muscular aches and strains. Some forms, such as Swedish massage, are intended as an alternative to exercise while others, such as shiatsu, are healing in their approach.

Meditation

Meditation can be broadly defined as any activity that keeps the attention pleasantly anchored in the present. When the mind is calm and focused in the present, it is neither reacting to memories of the past nor being preoccupied with plans for the future, two major sources of chronic stress known to impact health.

Meditation is a safe and simple way to balance a person's physical, emotional, and mental states. It is easily learned and has been used as an aid in treating stress and pain management. It has also been employed as part of an overall treatment for other conditions, including hypertension and heart disease (see the suggested meditations in Chapter 5).

Mind/body medicine

Mood, attitude and belief can affect virtually every chronic illness, and fear, cynicism, as well as a sense of hopelessness and helplessness, can have a detrimental effect on health. Courage, good humour, a sense of control, and hopefulness on the other hand can all be beneficial. Optimistic people are less likely to become ill and, when they do become ill, tend to live longer and suffer less. How well you *think* you are may be the best predictor of wellbeing and future health. Mind/body medicine may soon revolutionise modern health care. Recognising the profound interconnection of mind and body, the body's innate healing capabilities, and the role of self-responsibility in the healing process, mind/body medicine utilises a wide range of disciplines, including biofeedback, imagery, hypnotherapy, meditation and yoga.

Naturopathic medicine

Naturopathic medicine treats health conditions by utilising the body's inherent ability to heal. Naturopathic physicians aid the healing process by incorporating a variety of alternative methods – such as diet and clinical nutrition, homoeopathy, acupuncture, herbal medicine, hydrotherapy, therapeutic exercise, massage, physical therapies involving electric currents, ultrasound and light therapy, therapeutic counselling and pharmacology. Which of these are used is based on the patient's individual needs.

Neural therapy

Neural therapy uses injections of anaesthetics (into the nerve sites of the autonomic [independent] nervous system, acupuncture points, scars, glands, and other tissues) to remove short circuits in the body's electrical network. This process frees the body's flow of energy and normalises cellular function, making neural therapy an effective treatment for a variety of health conditions, especially chronic pain.

Neuro-Linguistic Programming

Neuro-Linguistic Programming focuses on how people learn, communicate, change, grow and heal. 'Neuro' refers to the way the brain works and how human thinking demonstrates consistent and detectable patterns. 'Linguistic' refers to the verbal and non-verbal expressions of the brain's thinking patterns. 'Programming' refers to how these patterns are recognised and understood by the mind and how they can be altered, allowing a person to make better choices in behaviour and health.

NLP has provided positive results for people suffering from various conditions, including AIDS, cancer, allergies, arthritis, Parkinson's disease and migraine headaches.

Nutritional supplements

Recent research has demonstrated that diet alone may not be sufficient to supply the nutrients necessary for overall good health. While most experts agree that nutritional supplements are vital in treating a variety of illnesses, injuries, and age-related problems, vitamin and mineral supplements can also help to maintain optimal physical and psychological health, promote longevity and prevent chronic disease.

Orthomolecular medicine

Even today many physicians disregard the value of proper nutrition in relation to health. The prevalent notion is that a balanced diet will provide all the nutrition one needs. What is overlooked, however, is the fact that much of the food supply in developed countries (especially in the United States) is processed and grown in nutritionally depleted soil. Orthomolecular physicians recognise these factors, as well as the fact that biochemical individuality can also play a crucial role in health.

Employing vitamins, minerals and amino acids to create optimum nutritional content and balance in the body, orthomolecular medicine targets a wide range of conditions, including depression, hypertension, schizophrenia, cancer and other mental and physiological disorders.

Osteopathy

Osteopathy considers and treats the patient as a whole rather than narrowly focusing on a specific ailment. It is a form of physical medicine that helps to restore the structural balance of the musculoskeletal system. Combining joint manipulation, physical therapy, and postural re-education, osteopathy is effective in treating spinal and joint difficulties, arthritis, digestive disorders, menstrual problems and chronic pain.

Oxygen therapy

Oxygen therapy refers to a wide range of therapies utilising oxygen in various forms to promote healing and destroy pathogens (disease producing micro-organisms and toxins) in the body. These therapies are grouped according to the type of chemical process involved: the addition of oxygen to the blood or tissues is called 'oxygenation,' and 'oxidation' is the reaction of splitting off electrons (electrically charged particles) from any chemical molecule. Oxidation may or may not involve oxygen (oxidation refers to the chemical reaction and not to oxygen itself).

Although various oxygen therapies have been utilised in Europe for many years for a wide range of conditions, in the United States most remain controversial and are currently unapproved by the Food and Drug Administration. Legality of oxygen therapies varies from state to state.

Reconstructive therapy

Reconstructive therapy uses injections of natural substances to stimulate the growth of connective tissue in order to strengthen weak or damaged tendons or ligaments. As a simple, economic alternative to drug and surgical treatments, reconstructive therapy is an effective treatment for degenerative arthritis, low back pain, carpal tunnel syndrome, migraine headaches, and torn ligaments and cartilage.

Sound therapy

The ability of sound and music to heal has been recognised for thousands of years. Sound therapists base their treatments on the fact that certain sounds can slow the breathing rate and create a feeling of overall wellbeing; other sounds can slow a racing heart, even soothe a restless baby. Sound can also alter skin temperature, reduce blood pressure and muscle tension, and influence brainwave frequencies. Although some sounds (like ultrasonic waves) are beyond the range of the human ear, they can have a profound effect on the human condition.

Sound therapy is used in hospitals, schools, corporate offices and psychological treatment programmes as an effective treatment to reduce stress, lower blood pressure, alleviate pain, overcome learning difficulties, improve movement and balance, and promote endurance and strength.

Traditional Chinese Medicine

Traditional Chinese Medicine (TCM) is an ancient method of health care that combines the use of medicinal herbs, acupuncture, food therapy, massage and therapeutic exercise. The philosophy of TCM is preventive and makes a point of educating the patient with regard to lifestyle so that the patient can assist in the self-healing process. The TCM practitioner educates the patient about diet, exercise, stress management, rest, and relaxation.

Yoga

Yoga means 'union': the integration of physical, mental and spiritual energies that enhance health and wellbeing. It was first written about by Patanjali in the second century BC in the Yoga Sutras. Yoga teaches a basic principle of mind/body unity: if the mind is chronically restless and agitated, the health of the body will be compromised, and if the body is in poor health, mental strength and clarity will be adversely affected. The practices of yoga can counter these ill effects, restoring mental and physical health. The most basic yoga is Hatha yoga which is a series of movements known as *asanas* (postures) designed to keep the body supple and fit. They can be quite simply learnt by anyone.

* * *

Obviously, it is beyond the scope of this book to describe all the therapies that can aid relaxation. Others you might like to check out are:

- Auto-suggestion
- Counselling
- Encounter groups
- Humanistic psychology
- Metamorphic technique
- Reflexology
- Reiki
- Rolfing
- Shiatsu
- T'ai chi

FURTHER READING AND RESOURCES

Craze, Richard, *Teach Yourself Alexander Technique*, Hodder & Stoughton, London, 1996.

Craze, Richard, *Teach Yourself Traditional Chinese Medicine*, Hodder & Stoughton, London, 1998.

Craze, Richard and Tang, Stephen, *Chinese Herbal Medicine*, Piatkus Books, 1995.

Foulkes, Jane, *Complementary Medicine Careers Handbook*, Hodder & Stoughton, London, 1991.

Lettvin, Maggie, *The Back Book*, Souvenir Press Ltd, London, 1976.

Mulligan, John, *The Personal Management Handbook: How To Make The Most Of Your Potential*. Sphere Books, London, 1988.

Ozaniec, Naomi, *Teach Yourself Meditation*, Hodder & Stoughton, London, 1997.

Powell, Trevor, *Free Yourself from Harmful Stress*, Dorling Kindersley, 1997.

Stanway, Dr Andrew, *Alternative Medicine: A Guide to Natural Therapies*. Bloomsbury Books, London, 1979.

Stewart, Mary, *Teach Yourself Yoga*, Hodder & Stoughton, 1998.

Weeks, Claire, *Self-help for Your Nerves*, Angus and Robertson, London, 1962.

World Wide Web

■ Short Relaxation Techniques – Sam Houston State University Counselling Centre. Short Relaxation Techniques
http://www.shsu.edu/~counsel/shortr.html

■ Relaxation Techniques – Relaxation Techniques. Pulmonary Rehabilitation Program, The Cheshire Medical Centre. General Guidelines.
http://www.cheshire-med.com/programs/pulrehab/rehman/relax.html

■ Relaxation Techniques for Relief of Anxiety & Stress – Health World Online – Relaxation Techniques for Relief of Anxiety & Stress.
http://healthy.net/library/books/lark/relax6.htm

■ MIDIRS books & videos – Relaxation techniques –
http://www.midirs.org/books/bs-rt.htm

■ Relaxation techniques – http://www.mid.co.uk/ecal/relaxation.html

■ Health Guide: Therapy – Relaxation Techniques – This site offers comprehensive, up-to-date information on psychological therapy.
http://healthguide.com/Therapy/relax.stm

■ Mind Tools – Effective Stress Management – Physical Relaxation Techniques – Mind Tools –
http://www.demon.co.uk/mindtool/smphyrel.html

■ Relaxation Techniques – Relaxation Techniques —
http://erm1.u-strasbg.fr/~keyser/dipl/node19.html

■ Mind Tools – Effective Stress Management – Physical Relaxation Techniques – Meditation. Taking Exercise. Physical relaxation techniques.
http://www.mindtools.com/smphyrel.html

■ SDS: Relaxation Techniques – Relaxation Techniques. Emergency Quick Relaxation Technique. Deep Breathing Exercises. Clearing Your Mind.
http://www.mis.ucg.ie/sds/relaxtech.html

■ Health Guide: Therapy – Relaxation Techniques – This site offers comprehensive, up-to-date information on psychological therapy.
http://www.healthguide.com/VTherapy/relax.stm

■ Health guide: Becoming A Mother – Relaxation Techniques –
http://www.healthguide.com/BeAMothr/relax.stm

■ Relaxation Techniques for Better Breathing – Relaxation Techniques for Better Breathing.
http://www.cchs.edu/AHP/relax.html

■ Relaxation Techniques (Alternative Medicine) – Relaxation Techniques - Alternative Medicine –
http://www.einet.net/galaxy/Medicine/Alternative-Medicine/Relaxation-Techniques.html

■ Relaxation techniques:
http://www.glasswing.com/~ibis/relaxati.html

■ Are There Any Basic Guidelines for Using Relaxation Techniques?
http://www.mediconsult.com/general/shareware/pain_control/nomeds_c.html

■ ACE Graphics – Relaxation Techniques
http://www.acegraphics.com.au/product/book/bk420.html

■ Meditation (Relaxation Techniques) –
http://www.einet.net/galaxy/Medicine/Alternative-Medicine/Relaxation-Techniques/Meditation.html

■ Statistical Relaxation Techniques –
http://opentech.olvit.ru/~abs/Lectures/arachnid.cs.cf.ac.uk/Dave/Vision_lecture/subsection2_1_9_1.html

■ Relaxation Techniques to Help You Sleep –
http://www.theglassceiling.com/archives/Health/herelax.htm

■ Relaxation Techniques – Sam Houston State University Counselling Centre.
http://www.shsu.edu/~counsel/relaxation.html

■ Effective Stress Management –
http://cis.paisley.ac.uk/scripts/staff.pl/will-ci0/MindSite/smphyrel.html

■ Relaxation Techniques – Magic Stream Relaxation Techniques: How to Meditate. Meditation. T'ai Chi. –
http://hawk-systems.com/web_pages/garson/relax.htm

■ Relaxation Techniques – Relaxation Techniques. Quick Relaxation:
http://wso.williams.edu/peerh/stress/relax.html

■ Exercise helps reduce stress better than relaxation techniques –
http://www.townonline.com/arlington/entertainment/health/029688_2_exercise_031197_57b1695656.html

- Relaxation Techniques – Audio Health Library. Relaxation Techniques. – http://yourhealth.com/ahl/1847.html
- Relaxation Techniques (Alternative Medicine) – http://lmc.einet.net:8000/galaxy/Medicine/Therapeutics/Alternative -Medicine/Relaxation-Techniques.html
- PAIN GAME: Relaxation Techniques – http://www.spine-dr.com/pain/paingame/pg.relax.html
- Harp Mailing List 1997 Archive: Relaxation techniques workshop http://tns-www.lcs.mit.edu/harp/archives/1997.07/0372.html
- WEB1 – Comparative Studies of Transcendental Meditation. http://www.erols.com/tmdelco/page7.html
- The Learning Link – General – Human Resources. Other Job Families. Job Family : General. Communication. Innovativeness/Initiative. Teamwork. Knowledge and Technical Skill. http://www.ucalgary.ca/UofC/departments/HR/LEARN/general.html
- Hatha Yoga-http://www.utexas.edu/student/txunion/iclass/Fall-1997/mind.html
- The Layman's Guide to the Dream World: Relaxation – Relaxation as a dream-tool – http://home.earthlink.net/~izone/tools/relax.htm

INDEX

TEACH YOURSELF

ALEXANDER TECHNIQUE

Do you have back problems? Would you like to learn a new approach to good health?

The Alexander Technique is a way of re-educating your body through realignment of the spine to give relief from pain and stress and an enhanced sense of well-being. First developed in the early part of the twentieth century it has taken its place as a major new therapy.

Richard Craze provides a practical, simple and effective guide using a series of practical exercises and procedures that you can try out for yourself. The book is illustrated with many fully labelled and informative diagrams.

Other titles available
Teach Yourself Massage
Teach Yourself Aromatherapy
Teach Yourself Yoga

TEACH YOURSELF

MEDITATION

Meditation is a traditional discipline which has been practised through the ages, and has long been recognised for its spiritual and restorative powers.

Teach Yourself Meditation introduces the theory and practice of meditation in a direct and simple manner. The book includes a variety of approaches, and compares the methods and goals of both Eastern and Western systems. With its holistic view of life, meditation can help you to gain a new perspective for the future.

About the author
Naomi Ozaniec has studied meditation for over ten years and has written several books on the subject.